Second Edition

COLLEGE
READING
Reading and Writing Collaboration

Anastasia Krueck-Frahn, M.Ed.

Kendall Hunt
publishing company

Cover image © Shutterstock.com

Kendall Hunt
publishing company

www.kendallhunt.com
Send all inquiries to:
4050 Westmark Drive
Dubuque, IA 52004-1840

Published in the United States of America

Contents

About me

My name is Anastasia Krueck-Frahn (Krick-Fron). Born and raised in Cleveland, Ohio, I have had the opportunity to experience a culturally diverse city. My family has played an intricate role in my own growth and development and my children are a major part of my life. They have enabled me to share my love of learning, of the arts, and of teaching. Now as adults, they have continued with their education, and used their degrees and post-secondary education to help them succeed.

My journey in education began traditionally, and continued much later as a non-traditional student. Personally, I believe everyone has the opportunity to learn, which is both reachable and attainable. From The University of Toledo, I earned both my Bachelor of Education and my Master of Education. In addition, I hold a State of Ohio Reading Endorsement, and the Licensure of Pre-K through Third grade.

Why write a textbook? "Reading and Writing: Skills that Go Together" became a passion I wanted to share with others. "College Reading: Reading and Writing Collaboration" takes a look past reading and ties the writer to design a social perspective that applies in the "real world." Education is a journey: you never know where it will take you until you decide to get on a path. Continuing any education is the key to success and there is much to learn from life.

Oddly, one of my all-time favorite things to do is to ponder thoughts. I feel through reflection, a person has the chance to improve their life, others' lives, and change the future. Very rarely, do people get second chances, so I make the most of it, if it happens.

A thought to ponder — "A pessimist sees the difficulty in every opportunity; an optimist sees the opportunity in every difficulty."

~Sir Winston Churchill

Acknowledgements

There are so many different people to thank for all of the wonderful advice, encouragement, and critiquing of my work. However, there are few people that deserve special recognition for the seamless ability to go above and beyond to help me succeed. These people make dreams come true, and guide without really taking credit. Nevertheless, remembering the drive to guide others, years of research and ability to believe in oneself has taken years to share with others.

Now on-to the Thank You's!

First, my family has always tried to support any crazy idea that I may have had to improve their lives or mine. Learning from their perspectives allowed me to put these skills into practice, as reading something comes in many forms. My desire to combine "reading and writing" became a lifelong project – Working with a concept and developing the knowledge learned to share with others that still needed to be taught the concept and value of reading. The "big picture" should be seen, because if you cannot see the end of something, what good is the beginning.

My mentors were instrumental in my success, in academics they came at two very different times in my life. Starting with my return to college as a nontraditional student with four very small children, and the other as my return to teach in a four-year institution. Both people came into my life with the understanding of a need and the ability to spark metacognition to excel at the production of a reading instrument.

Dr. Laurie Dinnebeil was a pillar of strength for me to succeed with many odds stacked against me, and she used her words to challenge views, beliefs and abilities helped create the educator I am today. Dr. Joyce Hall-Yates has been an active-participant throughout most of my teaching; however, she believed in my ability to see potential in students. She recognized students need to be able to read well in college and my desire of reading and writing as one skill became a project in 2015. There is a value to reading well, and students need every advantage to help them. Skills and strategies are priceless if applied correctly. Learn reading is a tool that is an ally not an enemy; enjoy learning there is a difference.

Preface: Welcome to College Reading

In this instructional guide, reading and writing have been combined, because one skill truly cannot function without the other. The more a person writes, edits, and revises their work, the more reading takes place. The more the reader reads, the better their writing will become.

There are countless opportunities for reading success. Reading can become bothersome, frustrating, and complicated, but learning is one of the most essential tools achieved from reading. These skills are fundamental and taught at a very early age, and now they can be relearned from a different perspective, and a chance to explore language at a new level.

Reading is something you need in everyday life. You may be shocked at the discovery of usage. Reading is very visual; collectively, most people do it and do not realize they have done it. For example, they read signs, pictures, text, colors, music, books, newspapers, movies, artwork, people, and so many other genres.

Reading is viewed as a complex series of interpretations that become very personal. The achievement of the skill is the comprehension with a deep and meaningful metacognition. Learning to collaborate and use discussion is the key to success in most courses and life in general; after all, communication is considered one of the keys to success. Finally, one must decide the complexity of interpretation, and "how to filter" out important details versus supports. These key details are needed to make the reading stronger, and articulate the topic or concept that the reader needs to learn. Allowing your personal vulnerability to see the perspective of someone else is the first step to opening your mind to new possibilities.

Continued use of skills and strategies throughout the course will help students to:

- Practice comprehension strategies to promote active reading.
- Practice writing strategies, and writing process as an extension of reading.
- Combine skills in activating prior background knowledge, group discussions, community collaboration, community service projects, and time management to enhance reading skill.
- Review reading and writing strategies, such as skimming, survey, question, reread, recite, purpose, tone, author intentionality, predictions, synopsis, the prologue, context, literary terms, vocabulary, brainstorming, clustering, listing, mapping, and outlining.
- Access key concepts of reading, such as denotation, connotation (inference), main idea, supporting details, thesis statement, topic sentence, and logic.
- Introduce visual literacy, integration of media, reading systems, elements of research, library orientation, information literacy, and critical thinking strategies to promote multiple perspectives.
- Introduce an onset of skills, such as note-taking, highlighting, concept cards, an association of text, annotation, imagery, key concepts, notations, bold text context, content clues, diction, evaluating text, and Cornell Notetaking.
- Introduce patterns of organization or thought patterns, such as time order, spatial, classification, chronological order, cause/effect, compare/contrast, example, process, definition, problem-solution, persuasion, argument, narration, and expository text.
- Develop language and literacy through context and parts of a text (written), parts of oral (spoken) statements as printed communication via discussion boards.

Once, the reader learns the ability to see things in context, question, and look for relevant information, they should be able to share their perception on the event, concept, or idea. Keep of mind, others have read the same source, and many people have several perspectives. Sharing this through discussion allows most people to see a clearer picture. These new points then become debates or "arguments," and the presentation of ideas becomes either implicit or explicit with details to support a point-of-view.

Lastly, the reader must recall information. Idealistically, they will be able to comprehend the concept, time, place, details, key people, events (history), and summarize knowledge to give an objective overview of "what just happened?" They must remember to transition their thoughts and assimilate the whole picture, not just part of it.

Being a reader is an important job. Knowing the difference between information as relevant or irrelevant will eliminate the falsification of that information, lead to a better recall of facts, and help develop a sound writing sample. The more you read, it will become easier; you should be able to read faster and retain the information read. Remember, this skill takes practice.

Remember, there are 10,000 reasons not to do something, you need to find one reason you should, and it will make the difference. Challenge your knowledge against past information and submerge your brain in language. Etymologies, the history of the information, are key, and do not forget that vocabulary is a "weapon," and it intimidates most people. Do not let language it intimidate you. Enjoy the journey; it is just another adventure waiting to happen. Open our book and begin the journey, reading and writing is a collaboration – they need each other.

Chapter 1

Active versus Passive Reader

Building Background and General Knowledge

Before we become better readers, an understanding of "the writer" must be understood. As background, knowledge and common sense begin to play an active role in our learning: Please remember this class is designed to be a "work in progress." Therefore, we will always be making progress in our work. Things to remember! As a student, you arrive in a university setting with preconceived notions, expectations, and plans in mind. However, please remember, as our class is culturally diverse, the "common knowledge" will become diminished and in turn will become replaced by a common respect for people, especially for those placed in our classroom, and our campus.

Therefore, the subject matter may cause some uncomfortable moments, feelings, or even false perceptions, as in an academic setting students should begin to critically think different situations through, until they have arrived at multiple perspectives of the topic, main idea, or concept being introduced within the course. Remember, academics are here to guide us to "think," especially critically. Consequently, we will begin to expand one perspective into the possibility of many views. More importantly, we will begin to guide you through an evolution of thought – learning that should be reflective in nature. Most of the time, this process requires the facilitator to take you on a journey to enhance knowledge using many types of genre, to expose your mind into developing accurately many interpretations throughout several disciplines found within a higher education.

Although we may not enjoy all types of genre, the exposure, understanding, purpose, intentionality, and culture guide us to a stronger understanding of content. For the same reason, it could be said that the interpretation could solely lead a reader inadvertently to misinterpret the context as the process of sending and receiving within our cognitive ability could be limited based on perception and background knowledge we have learned over our lifetime. Keeping this in mind, our limits could lead to hurt feelings, or misunderstanding within our classroom; remember culture influences everything. Lastly, the mindset we place ourselves will promote our ability to learn, whereas an open mind will be evaluating with multiple perspectives. Accepting differences of opinions and respect of human interests will help ensure overall success in many facets of your life. As a result, if you tell yourself, "you can't – you won't." On the other hand, if you tell yourself, "I'll try – you just might succeed." Perseverance is one of the keys to success, making mistakes is one of the best ways to learn, as long as you always reflect on the situation. Moving forward, stay positive, open-minded, embrace challenges, and learn, then you can make a difference in education and to your future.

Introductory Discussion

About Discussion Board Posts

In this course, you will be interacting on a regular basis throughout the term on Discussion Boards. There will be at least one or two Discussion Board assignments throughout the following weeks. On each Discussion Board, you are responsible for two different kinds of posts: *Initial posts* and *Secondary posts*. All discussion board posts are **semi-formal**, which means they should be spell-checked and organized. In other words, your Discussion Board post **should not** be a first draft. After you type your Discussion Board post, re-read it to make sure you have not made any significant grammar/spelling errors and, most importantly, to make sure it expresses your ideas in a way that will be easy for readers to understand.

Initial posts are your main contribution to the class discussion. These posts are listed on the syllabus, and should be at least 200 words in length (unless otherwise noted). Each initial post should make a thoughtful contribution to the conversation. Secondary posts are shorter responses to the initial posts written by your classmates.

You are expected to write at least two secondary posts that are more than 100 words in length (unless otherwise noted) for each Discussion Board assignment. In short, for each week, you will be required to interact on two Discussion Board assignments, which means that you will write at least two initial posts (200+ words each) and four secondary posts (100+ words each) each week for our course. To give you a sense of length, the following paragraph is of 213 words:

Welcome to the Introductory Discussion Board Assignment

Doing academic reading and writing is hard work. In this class, we will be doing much of that work together through collaborative discussion boards and by sharing our own work with one another in various ways. Learning academic writing will require us all to share our thoughts and ideas through writing, to read critically each other's work, to ask questions, and to share successful strategies for reading and writing at the college level. Often times, it can be difficult to share our writing – we work hard on our writing, and many of us hold strong feelings that we have written our responses as best as we could. One challenge that writers face is to learn how to be open to the constructive criticism offered by others. To support this development, the goal of the class is to create a sense of community in which we feel comfortable enough to discuss openly our ideas and to critique, or analyze, comment on, review each other's written work. This introductory discussion board assignment will help us to begin creating a sense of community by allowing us to meet one another and begin to talk about reading and writing at the college level. The better we know each other, the easier it will be to work together over the next 15 weeks!

Overview

Over the next 15 weeks, we are going to talk to each other a lot about reading, writing and more writing! In order to make this a successful class, we have to develop healthy working relationships with one another. Today we are going to begin to build those relationships by establishing a sense of community on this Introductory Discussion Board.

Discussion Focus – All About Me

Initial Post

Post is an initial response that addresses the following questions: Who are you? Tell us your name, where you are from, why you have come to a university for an education, and what you hope to do with that education. Describe the area you live in and the members of your immediate family. Tell us what you like to do on your free time.

Answer one of these icebreaker questions:

- If you could be a cereal-box character for just 24 hours, which one would you choose and why?
- What was the most important thing to you as a child? As a teenager? Now? Explain why you think these things have changed (or stayed the same).
- If you could work for a circus, what would your job be and why?
- You were just given a yacht. What will you name it? Why?
- What cartoon character best represents your personal philosophy? Why?

Secondary Posts

Respond to your peers by asking questions and drawing connections with your own experiences. Guidelines are that you must respond to at least two peers, or in other words to your classmates with a minimum written response of 100 words per classmate. The length is as important as engagement and interaction are important; therefore, adding from your peer's original post will help expand your secondary response in the discussion board.

Completing This Task

To Post Your Initial Response:

1. Click the **Respond** button below.
2. On the Respond screen, enter a descriptive title in the Subject area, and type your posting in the Message box.
3. Answer the question(s) in complete sentences. Be as detailed as possible to answer the prompt thoroughly.
4. Be sure to check your spelling, grammar, and punctuation. (Note: You can also type your answer into a word processor and copy and paste it into the Message screen. This will also help to check your word count.)
5. Click the **Post to forum** button to submit your posting.

To Post Follow-up Responses to Your Peers:

1. On the original discussion screen, postings will appear below at the bottom of page. Choose the posting that you want to reply to by clicking on its title.

2. The posting will open on another screen. Click the **Reply** link in the lower right-hand corner of the posting.
3. The Editing screen will appear. Please note that the title is already filled in from your peer's original posting. This is how the system keeps track of the discussion threads. Type your response in the Message box. Be sure to check your spelling, grammar, and punctuation.
4. Click the **Post to forum** button to submit your response.

Assessment and Grading

Writing Requirements – see rubric in Chapter 3

Due Tuesday 11:59 p.m.

- Initial Post Length: 150–200 words

Due Sunday 11:59 p.m.

- Secondary Post Length: minimum of 100 words per post (respond to at least two peers or in other words to your classmates)

Writing Strategies

As many of you begin this course, you may say, "I write really well," and some of you probably have some good strategies to help with the writing process. Nevertheless, the following strategies will be utilized throughout this course, and should be applied across the curriculum in all aspects of writing in academic disciplines (especially your courses selected to complete your degree program). Just as importantly, it is advantageous for your college career to use as many strategies needed to succeed your overall growth in education.

With that being said, concepts of brainstorming, a replica of a basic outline, a guide and some hyperlinks, and the library are great resources and they should become part of your daily routine while accomplishing reading and writing tasks. Please remember, these strategies are collectively utilized throughout your educational process and do not promote exclusivity to "just this class." Keep in mind, all materials are covered in class, and guides help to keep you organized in your academic studies.

Basic Writing Strategies

Brainstorm

Brainstorming is similar to a "freewrite," except that there is more structure to the writing sample. For instance, the use of a list is one of the most common techniques to "brainstorming"; second, the use of questions, or directed writing, as the question becomes directly answered within the sample. The next logical transition from "brainstorming" becomes either the "outline, or the rough draft." Remember, as you are asking questions, do not use a question word unless it is truly a "question." Common question words to use in writing are "where, who, and when." Although these words are used in everyday common language, better words to use in writing would be that, this, and there.

Brainstorming can help you choose a topic, develop an approach to a topic, or deepen your understanding of the topic's potential. Samples of brainstorming are: freewrite, list, cluster, or take notes as directed by your instructor. Outlines are more detailed, placed in order of importance, and used to create organization of thoughts, patterns, and overall perspective throughout your writing sample.

Freewrite

Freewriting is an example of writing on particular thoughts or notions for which the topic at hand must become expanded into a writing sample. Therefore, usually 10–15 minutes of uninterrupted time must be spent on compiling of information to create the sample. Consequently, the writing sample itself may look like nothing more than a compilation of "words and sentences" that really "have no connection" or collocation to one another. In particular, the sentences lack transition and the paragraphs have multiple topics hidden with them.

Idealistically, the freewrite will eliminate the need for proper grammar and mechanical structure found within the sentences or paragraphs. Therefore, the writing will have an array of "misspelled" words, run-on sentences, or horrible fragments to represent "thoughts." However, the least restrictive the writing is, the more "imagination" you will be able to incorporate into the writing sample itself, which in turn will allow the "most freedom" toward writing an assignment.

Freewriting is an opportunity to let creativity flow, as you take pen and paper, or simply begin typing on a keyboard or tablet as you produce. Freewriting is a simple process to explore different topics, ideas, and thoughts, all in one place. Whenever you freewrite, set a timer to write freely anything that comes to your mind, as grammar, sentence structure, or even coherence will be overlooked. This is one of the best "brainstorming strategies" to help with creativity in writing. This strategy will help eliminate "writers block." For all intended purposes of writing, this strategy is as a "babble" without an end, and the ideas are limitless. This strategy is used before a rough draft.

List

Listing is a good strategy, again similar to "freewriting" as there is no rhyme or reason for the list. You will just record in text, the ideas, topics, or key points you would like in your writing sample. One way to think of "list" is to compare it with a list needed for a trip or to the grocery store, or "Santa's list" as you will check twice to make sure all the key points and ideas have been recorded before the rough draft.

Outline

Outlining has two "typical" forms that most students associate with writing: first, a "topic outline" and second, a "sentence outline." As you begin to write out your outline, regardless of the choice of "outline," you must remember the "golden rule." All outlines are formal; therefore have a specific style, which does not vary from outline to outline. If your outline contains a "Roman Numeral I," then your outline must contain a "Roman Numeral II." If your outline contains a "Capital A, then a Capital B" must follow the format. If your outline contains a "number 1, then a number 2" must follow the format. All items must be placed in pairs, or they stand alone; you may not have an A without a B, or a 1 without a 2, and so forth.

Remember all outlines must be delivered into the organizational format as the pairs of Numerical/Alphabetical Portion or the "point" stands alone, which will include only the "category." The following example is a basic outline.

Title and Author (centered)

Thesis Statement:
- I. Introduction
  - A. One point
  - B. Two points
- II. Body
- III. Conclusion
  - A. One pint
  - B. Two points
    1. First, detail
    2. Second detail
       a. Minor detail
       b. Minor detail
          i. Supports minor detail
          ii. Supports minor detail

The Cluster

Clustering is taking the writing sample and making a "map or concept" into a more visible picture as you begin leading from the main idea or claim to the "bigger picture." Therefore, beginning "just like the outline," the title and author become the center of the "map." Other forms or cluster focus on individual topics or schemes to give the reader and writer a clearer picture to overall transition that may occur from "one idea to the next." Some writers may refer to this concept as a "web," whereas it will begin to take the shape of a "spider web."

Clustering is another way to think of new ideas. The word "cluster" means a group of similar things. Clustering means putting words into groups. Each group, or cluster, has a number of words placed into groupings or categories related to each other. Clustering is similar to outlining. You try to think of many words and phrases. As you make a cluster map, you write the words and phrases in groups. Here is an example of a cluster map:

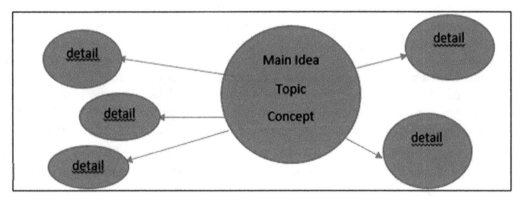

Created by Anastasia Krueck-Frahn

Writing Worksheet

The assignment as you write must have pertinent information about your assignment, including the title, point of view, source(s) if reading-based, audience, writing pattern (if any), length, whether to include a rough draft or revised drafts, and whether your paper must be typed, or written. All information read need to be accurately written. Staying on the topic at hand, or the current task, from the beginning of the thesis is different from a "topic sentence." The thesis can be located in any sentence in the introduction paragraph, and typically will be the longest sentence along with containing all supporting information on your chosen concept, topic, or idea that will give credibility to your point-of-view; in addition, it will be very comprehensive.

Strategies to explore concepts

Freewrite, list, brainstorm, cluster, or take notes (annotated notation) as directed by your instructor.

Get Organized Fast

Use a starting point, whether you brainstorm or freewrite (everything you know with no limits, order of true functions, or sense to right or wrong); make a list or base everything from a lecture. Next step, get yourself organized fast. Begin with an outline; whether it is formal or informal to create some logic to your writing sample. Remember, there is a difference between the two outlines, but the requirement is the instructor's choice, but if not required strongly recommended because the results of your work will be reflected in the process. Now, write a topic sentence (get the reader's attention) and a thesis, which will label the subject and focus on the parts of the writing sample. Write an outline or a structured, detailed list. For reading-based writing, include references and short quotations with page numbers as a quick "look back" to support your final sample in the outline or list.

On a Roll

Different requirements to polish your work

Write, revise, edit, reread, rewrite, read it backwards, and proof it (spell checker or grammarly); finally, read aloud (recommended two copies – one for you and one for your reader: hear it).

On separate paper, write the first step to your final product that begins the rough draft. Revise your work as many times as necessary. A good essay becomes a great essay once takes reflection and improvement, because majority of people just do not get it right once. Now, check your work for coherence, do transition in your thoughts, paragraphs or even sentences to make your sample flow throughout the work. Remember, use academic language unless informal is acceptable. The usage of language, the diction, etymology of your word choices, and the tone will set the readability to your piece. Finally, create a unity of your topic and keep like supports together (do not make the reader "dizzy"), emphasis on details, the credible support, and the sentence syntax, all the readers to become part of your perspective.

Now, finish your product. Make all basic edits to the fundamentals of writing text, such as grammar, punctuation, capitalization, spelling (does not change the meaning of the sentence); remember "hear" your words. Do not write "like you speak." This is not writing. This conversation there is no one asking you, "What do you mean?" Overall, your ability to "tell" someone clearly means you must disseminate the information accurately. Once you gain your chance to present your point-of-view, this knowledge typically requires support (do not forget – in-text citations, which will prevent plagiarism).

Discussion 2

As you begin this week, we will be exploring several strategies of reading and writing as discussions, activities, and assignments. For this discussion, please focus on the following questions as discussed in our class. Why do you read? Whom do you do homework for, you or someone else?

As you **reflect** on the questions, please begin your initial post with strategies that have made you successful in school, and please reflect on those strategies that were used in school that may not have been your best choice. Please read the following example of an initial post for the discussion board.

Reading is something that I have always enjoyed doing, especially if I read for entertainment, as I enjoy reading novels based on "suspense writing or murder mystery." I have learned if I am interested in a book to read, I tend to read it all the way to the end. However, if I read about a topic that I may not be interested in, hopefully, I will make it to the end of the reading. Some strategies I used in school included taking short breaks in-between reading technical information. Another would be to make note cards so that I could remember some of the information I was being taught, especially in science class. Whereas, there were too many terms to learn. As far as homework, I have learned that I am the one that will benefit from doing the extensions on concepts being introduced in the different subjects, therefore, it may take hours, but if I do not invest in me…who will.

Initial Post

150–200 words based on your perspective on the topics of reading, learning, strategies, homework, and overall view on success. The initial post will be after you take the time to prewrite as this may help alleviate writers block as you reflect on the past. One of the reasons to prewrite before making an initial post is it will give you an idea of your experiences in school.

When you write your initial post, use freewriting techniques to develop supporting details related to your chosen topic. When you freewrite, the aim is just to put your ideas down in writing – grammar and sentence structure do not matter in a freewrite. Instead, the most important objective of freewriting is to come up with new ideas, examples, details, explanations that help you develop a better understanding of your chosen topic. Remember the initial post is not a prewrite, therefore you will have to take the time to edit your grammar, spelling, format, and sentence structure as these count toward grading.

Prewriting

There are three important rules to help you be productive when freewriting:

1. **Never stop writing:** Even if you feel like you have run out of things to say, just write a sentence stating the topic until new thoughts emerge. For example, you might write this statement repeatedly when freewriting about family gatherings: "What else can I say about family gatherings? What else can I say about family gatherings? What else can I say about family? …"
2. **Never censor yourself:** Even if you feel like your ideas are stupid, irrelevant, unimportant, or that you cannot find the right words, just keep writing. Once you are done with the freewrite, you can go back and decide which ideas are useful, and which ideas are not useful. During the course of freewriting, do not stop writing even when you cannot find the right word; you know you spelled something wrong, or you think now that your ideas do not make sense.

3. **Write for a short period of time:** It will be difficult to sustain your attention while freewriting, so set short periods – at first, only 5 minutes. With practice, you may be able to freewrite for 10 minutes or more.

Secondary Posts

100 words each for at least two or more peers or classmates in the discussion board. For the secondary post, please review your peer's strategies and concept of reading and learning. Is their point-of-view understood in the writing sample? If you agree with your peer, please state why you agree; consequently, if you disagree please state why. For example, Jane as you stated, "I like to stay up late and watch TV, this was not a good strategy to try and complete my homework." I could relate, as I would find myself watching television instead of completing the assignments. I have since then learned that the programs have to wait, as the concepts being taught usually always build on one another.

Remember, try to make a connection with a peer, as you are a learning community. The support, understanding, and commonality you establish will become a strength for your coursework, in addition to the friendships and networking you would have achieved in your college years to come.

Writing Requirements (APA format)

- **Initial post:** 150–200 words
- **Secondary posts:** 100 words each for at least two or more peers
- 1-inch margins
- Double-spaced
- 12-point Times New Roman font
- Due date: Initial post – Wednesday before 11:59 p.m.
- Due date: All secondary posts – Sunday before 11:59 p.m.

**Grading is 0% if no submission, else is 5% for submission (5 points) – correct criterion will earn 5 points

Oops…to Read or to Read – Do it Engage the Brain

In our American society, some people have come to expect everything "right now." However, in reading, the person obtaining information from the text must understand that this is a process. In other words, one should not be finished quickly. For this purpose, all reading materials should be read actively and at various speeds depending on text, context, engagement, purpose, process, and knowledge being extracted for a common goal. For all intended purposes, we need to clarify with the material we have just read.

As for the emerging need for instant, quick, and often segmented words becoming the "norm" for modern language, this will not be tolerated. For example, the use of the cell phone has encouraged the need to create a "short-hand" form of language replacing words, such as "you" with the letter "u" or the proper noun "I" with a lower case "i." In this class and throughout your college career, the acceptance of American culture for spelling of products, places, and formal names without following the rules of English, as easily represented in words such as "ketchup, or katz" will not be accepted. Therefore, representing the English language should not be based on acronyms but rather the full words, which eliminates misinterpretation of the language being written or spoken (Joseph, 2007).

Nevertheless, culturally speaking, we have become passive readers; however, in order to learn and learn over time, we must become active readers. So, "What is the difference, we are 'reading' right?" Students have said, "I read it and I cannot remember a thing I read." Did they actually read it? Yes, figuratively speaking they took the time necessary to accomplish the "task of reading," but as you are reading you need to "take away" the meanings of passages, intention of an author, purpose of the writing, and the ability to put the material on a shelf; then say, "I understand."

Active reading begins and ends with the student fully engaged intellectually with the text. The use of reading strategies, such as prereading, vocabulary usage, prior knowledge, background knowledge, annotation, summaries, outlining, evaluating the text, and questioning the author's intention, besides the text. Make time to annotate the material in the margins of your article or book while reading. Relate these topics to real-world events, family events, or just simply ask, "what if." The real-life connection allows better recognition to a common topic being comprehended for future usage in discussion, recall, or writing down information. Now, "close the book," turn over the material, and ask questions – how, who, what, where, when, and why…no clue, time to read it again.

Remember to focus on patterns, take a "walk" through the book, look for vocabulary (familiar and unfamiliar words), read in a cursory fashion, question everything read, and use the survey of the passage to your advantage. Questions that you ask should emphasize your ability to critical thinking, and emerge yourself in an academic culture. (See yourself as a learner!) Overtime, you will begin to develop relationships between your diverse life experiences and the academic classroom; the continued practice of reading and writing with the strategies of learning will be significantly beneficial to a community of learners, as opposed to just being assigned the work and completing the task.

Assignment

Outline

For this assignment, please refer the reading from our chosen piece and outline the reading. Please remember to add key points that will be beneficial to you. In addition, outlining has two "typical" forms that most students associate with writing: first, a "topic outline" and second, a "sentence outline." As you begin to write out your outline, regardless of the choice of "outline," you must remember the "golden rule." All outlines are formal; therefore have a specific style, which does not vary from outline to outline. If your outline contains a "Roman Numeral I," then your outline must contain a "Roman Numeral II." If your outline contains a "Capital A, then a Capital B" must follow the format. If your outline contains a "number 1, then a number 2" must follow the format. All items must be placed in pairs, or they stand alone; you may not have an A without a B, or a 1 without a 2, and so forth.

The following is just an example of a basic outline (Your outline may contain more supports).

Title and Author (centered)

Thesis Statement:

    I. Introduction
       A. One point
       B. Two points
   II. Body
  III. Conclusion
       A. One point
       B. Two points
          1. First (major) detail
          2. Second (major) detail
             a. Minor detail
             b. Minor detail
                i. Supports minor detail
                ii. Supports minor detail

Remember all outlines must be delivered into the organizational format as the pairs of Numerical/Alphabetical Portion or the "point" stands alone, which will include only the "category."

Assessment and Grading

Upload Work to the Appropriate Area**

Writing Requirements (APA format)

- 1 to 2 pages (approximately 300 words per page)
- 1-inch margins
- Double-spaced
- 12-point Times New Roman font
- Due date: Sunday before 11:59 p.m.

**Grading is 0% if no submission, else 15% submission (15 points) – correct criterion will earn 15 points

Chapter 2

Reading – Titles/Subtitles

Prior Knowledge/Activating Background Knowledge

In academic writing, college reading becomes one of the key factors to develop success in college. Activating prior knowledge and developing more background knowledge are two skills that are often viewed as one process; however, background knowledge is a process that allows a student to dig deeper into subject matter, whereas they lacked or had little prior knowledge of a given topic as they never had being exposed to the topic, subject, or concept. Hence, we constantly are confronted, introduced, and exposed to new information, particularly as we progress to the upper elementary grades and beyond. In simpler terms, beginning from the third grade, there is the transition from "learning to read" to "reading to learn."

As students progress through different reading strategies and assimilation begins, a vast understanding of knowledge will shape reading and writing foundations that are needed for skills to become transferred from one discipline to another, then finally real-world applications. In "Inventing the University," Bartholomae (1986) noted that everyone makes accommodations depending on the situation. Reading and writing are no different.

In short, the terms "background knowledge" and "prior knowledge" are "themselves parent terms for many more specific knowledge dimensions" such as conceptual knowledge (abstract thought to knowing a concept) and metacognitive knowledge (the process of thinking about "how we think" on given topics). Consequently, the different types of subject matter knowledge (good at math), strategy knowledge (finish a task – process), personal knowledge (happened to me), and self-knowledge (look what I found) are all specialized forms of prior knowledge and background knowledge (Cunningham, Cunningham, Allington, & Hall, 2002).

Nevertheless, there is a well-established correlation between prior knowledge and reading comprehension and background knowledge, which can significantly improve students' comprehension of relevant reading material. In particular, you have important background ideas for an expository or narrative text, which in turn will lead to significantly greater performance on comprehension questions than if you had no "prereading" background knowledge.

Activating Background Knowledge

Some of the most common strategies we have to practice while activating background knowledge are the use of prompts (activate thoughts), orally stating the idea, writing down the concept, or recording it for later use. This information will be helpful in completing a task or writing an essay. For example, asking yourself to answer a simple question such as, "What do I already know about this topic" orally or even writing on paper is a straightforward way to activate knowledge (Carr & Thompson, 1996). Please keep in mind, I am not asking you to converse with yourself, so to speak, but I am asking you to question yourself. The deeper you dig to retrieve "what you already know," the more you will comprehend "what you need to know."

We assume that we have the ability to recall or strengthen comprehension simply by making a personal connection to the text, subject, idea, concept, or topic. Barrs (2000) found that activating background knowledge through reflection and oral elaboration during text reading tended to be some of the best strategies (p. 58). Then, activating relevant prior knowledge by expressing it in some form of what you already know about a topic has been demonstrated to be more effective than activating irrelevant background knowledge (opinions) (Carr & Thompson, 1996; Barrs, 2000; Cunningham, Cunningham, Allington, & Hall, 2002).

Practice a strategy. One tool to use would be a technique to collect information in a chart format for comparative information, such as What do you know? What do you want to know? What have you just learned after research? Commonly known as the KWL chart, maybe you recognize this strategy as some of your teachers may have used this technique in elementary school or high school, as they were helping you think "critically," develop background knowledge, and establish future "prior knowledge." Test the theory using the word "dog" on a piece of paper, recreate the chart, and fill in the blanks. Use prior knowledge to establish a good start and research areas of the subject you do not know to create more background knowledge. Now, peruse all that knowledge. Remember, this is a process; therefore, the more you practice some strategies, the stronger your skills will become "to do" just about anything. Below is an example of the chart.

DOG (topic)

What I Know	What I Want to Know	What I Learned

Discussion 1

For this discussion, we will be focusing on culture, backgrounds, and gender. As we came into the world, we received our gender and our birth name. Throughout the years, there was a possibility we would consider changing maybe one or possibly even both of them. However, our culture played an intricate role on our final decision. Consequently, "What's in a Name?" Atwan (2013) depicts that our attitudes may be "affected" by our name: "Is it fair to judge people by their names?" Yet, research conducted on "the brain" indicated that regardless of a person "liking their name or not," the likability was processed based on the easy pronunciation of a name. In fact, the "more pronounceable a person's name is, the more likely people are to favor them" (p. 47). According to Mosher (2012), "Easily Pronounced Names May Make People More Likeable" stated that "fluency" was the key as the "brain favors information that's easy to use" (p. 49). A correlation could be tied to the fluency of the reading and writing, similar to, if the passage being read is completed with fluency, the more likely a person will remember the content.

Furthermore, throughout history, names created an identity, influenced outcomes, presented a personification, influenced our personality, and affected our perceptions. However, there are many different reasons as to "why" we make judgments about each other. Personal appearance followed by personality, typically, is the first impression of someone, even before we know their name. "Studies have shown, for example, that people can partly predict a person's income and education using only their first name… and the less popular a name is, the more likely a child is to be delinquent" (Mosher, 2012, p. 50).

Initial Post

(150–200 words) Consider carefully. First, please reflect on your name, friend's name, or family name and post if you feel that the name is easy to remember because of its pronunciation. Secondly, please give attributes of the person in a short scenario or example that proves your theory. Finally, reflect on why you assume that these attributes may be closely tied to the person's name.

Please read the following example:

Every Christmas was the best at Uncle Bob's house as his was the largest in the family. Even at family events everyone always seemed to gather around Uncle Bob; he appeared to be the life of the party and the best storyteller. However, his wife, poor Aunt Martha, seemed always to stand in a corner of the room away from everyone, odd as she seemed to be a nice person. The reason could be that Uncle Bob owned his own business, seemed to be the "go to person," and genuinely "all around nice person."

Secondary Posts

(100 words each with at least two or more classmates) As you read your classmates' posts, does their "story" seem possible? If it does, please find at least one or two sentences that support your interpretation. Please remember to use in-text citation for either the quoted or the paraphrased material you incorporate into your post. For example, the following model might be used. According to Mosher (2012), "Robert" was listed on the "top 10 baby names of the 1970s" and it would make sense that "Uncle Bob" would appear to be one of the most successful in the family (p. 51). In fact, "Altogether the researchers found that a name's pronounceability, regardless of length or seeming foreignness, mattered most in determining likability" (Mosher, 2012, p. 50).

Writing Requirements (American Psychological Association [APA] format)

- **Initial post:** 150–200 words
- **Secondary posts:** 100 words each for at least two or more peers
- 1-inch margins
- Double spaced
- 12-point Times New Roman font
- Due date: Initial post – Tuesday before 11:59 p.m.
- Due date: All secondary posts – Sunday before 11:59 p.m.

**Grading is 0% no submission or is 5% submission (5 points) – correct criterion will earn 5 points

General Reading

Reading is a fundamental skill acquired throughout several different stages of our life. Somewhere along the line the skill was lost or not developed properly; it could have been hindered by a lack of interest, possibly a developmental delay or lack of enrichment for cognition, or even a disability that prohibited the overall process to be thoroughly established over time. Reading itself is viewed as a concept that displays several meanings and holds various definitions based on word usage and contextual meaning; concurrently, according to Merriam-Webster, the definition reflects two meanings: first, "material read for or reading" and, secondly, "a particular interpretation of something," whereas readers, you will look at both definitions in depth.

Naturally, several reading strategies will need to be "reintroduced" into your daily learning and studying habits to ensure success during your educational journey. At the same time, we will need to learn the incorporation of practice of the strategies, so they become as natural as "brushing your teeth." Specifically, learning the difference between cursory reading and in-depth reading is needed for comprehension, because both skills have a very different purpose for comprehension.

Altogether, the skills, strategies, and practice of reading itself will promote necessary skills to use in the course and beyond; however, a cautionary note, this course will not "magically" improve your reading, as you will need to learn "how to adapt" these practices into your learning style. Eventually, if you put into practice, research supports an increase in reading comprehension, vocabulary development, and improved study habits.

Let's focus on the words "titles and subtitles" as these have an amazing feature in writing. First, the title should reflect the content being discussed in a reading, essay, summary, or other literary work. Second, the subtitles should reflect extensions of the content found within the paragraphs that follow, which in turn support the title. Even though the title and subtitles should accurately reflect the literary work, simultaneously, the title and subtitles become predictors. Through the prediction of the piece, the reader has the ability to think critically about the material, topic, task, or concept. Therefore, we begin to recall knowledge, utilize prior knowledge, and create an opportunity to develop background knowledge – all of which are necessary for comprehension. In addition, we have the opportunity to develop questions, ask questions, and create hypothesis as to the possible outcome. Again, these strategies are necessary for comprehension.

Equally important will be the skills learned over the duration of the course and, in particular, the skills introduced in Chapter 3. Again, as most of these skills require adaption to your learning style and, most importantly, practice, the suggestion to use them in all courses will create a stronger practice of learning each skill, and in turn develop a "good learning habit." Some of the strategies being introduced will be the use of prediction, facts versus opinions, purpose and tone, writing strategies, concept cards, the SQ4R (Survey, Question, Read, Recite, Relate and Review), extensive writing, vocabulary development (etymology, recognition, and usage), annotation, highlighting, note taking, context clues, pictures, diagrams, charts, "time management," and "Cornell Note Taking." For this week, we will primarily focus on the use of prediction and surveying the text.

Besides all of these topics given in an overview, learn to read everything, practice with license plates, street signs, and menus. A good "trick of comprehension": If we are able to close our eyes, write down "what we thought we saw," and get it correctly as we verify the information either verbally or visually, consequently, we are stretching our brain and developing stronger "recall skills" used in our memory.

In spite of everything, we are here in our collaborative community for a reason; most of the time a reason may be clearly understood, and yet for others, the reason may unfold at a later date or possibly in the near future. Regardless of the reason, we are glad you will have the opportunity to improve your reading, writing, and skills level to promote a greater chance for success within our university. In the end, the skills, strategies, and practice are all interconnected, and so let's get reading.

Plagiarism/How to Avoid It

Please note that throughout several of our lectures, you may have noticed while reading the information throughout the text, either in the beginning of the text, throughout one line, or even at the end, which was represented by odd names placed into parentheses. If you are not familiar as to "why" they were there, these pieces of necessary notations are called in-text citations. Collectively, their use is very simple: eliminate plagiarism. If we look at the term a different way, at the end of the lectures, you may have noticed a citation, source, or reference (author, date, title, etc....) at the bottom of the page. All I did was take the required format of the APA style and place the citation within the text. Hence, an in-text citation was created to notify the reader, "I have a thought, but it came from someone else." In fact, if I were using the Modern Language Association (MLA) style, the notation within the text and works cited at the end would look very different, but the purpose of the notation would be the same.

Often, there are misconceptions for the use of in-text citations, which are needed to eliminate plagiarism. More likely than not, you had a preconceived notion from your high school teacher as they may have said, "Please do not tell me where the information came from in the reading, I gave it to you." The teacher's knowledge of the content or subject matter was something they already knew, and their misunderstanding of "teaching" us the proper way of recording it onto paper might have been overlooked. Nevertheless, this advice has led to much confusion in a postsecondary setting (college setting), as in academia knowledge is "everything" and giving proper credit for this knowledge is the only ethical thing to do. We must give credit, where credit is due.

To put it differently, as plagiarism is created within our essays, discussions, and other tasks, we have confusion and questions, such as "I used my own words," or "You told me the reading, why don't you know where I got it?" Regardless, you must use in-text citation, along with the proper style of APA format for this class, or other courses may use MLA format, and please make sure to ask your other instructors, as they are similar, but they do have several differences in their style.

According to the APA and MLA guidelines, here are some indicators to help you as you write essays and give credit for information on a topic, idea, or concept required for your courses.

You want to give credit, where credit is due or you lose

Again, the key to avoiding plagiarism is to make sure you give credit where it is due. Remember, this may be credit for something somebody said, wrote, e-mailed, drew, or implied. Many professional organizations, including the MLA, APA, and the Chicago Manual of Style (CMS), have lengthy guidelines for citing sources. However, we are often so busy trying to learn the rules of MLA format and style or APA format and style that they sometimes accidentally forget exactly the types of documentation or credit that needs citing/notation.

Below is a brief list; therefore, every scenario we may come across in our academic writing samples may be missing or not listed as suggestions to avoid plagiarism. Remember, there are several other genres and topics not being credited or documented here:

- Words or ideas presented in any type of genre, commonly a blog, wiki, magazine, book, newspaper, journal, TV program, movie, information from a Web page, computer program, letter, advertisement, slogan, music, lyric, song, jingle (which will produce earworms or stuff that gets stuck in your brain that you cannot get rid of)
- Knowledge you gain through interviewing or conversing with another person, face to face, over the phone, or in writing (text or print)
- Copying the exact words or a unique phrase (offset the text with quotation marks)
- Reprinting any diagrams, illustrations, charts, pictures, or other visual materials
- Reusing or reposting any electronically available media, including images, audio, video, or other media (podcast, YouTube)

Consequently, the bottom line is document any words, ideas, or other information that originates somewhere outside of you. Remember, even if you have general knowledge of an idea, topic, or thought, once you are exposed to others' writing on the subject, you must give them credit.

There are, of course, certain things that do not need documentation or credit; some of these points, thoughts, or topics include:

- Writing your own lived experiences, your own observations and insights, your own thoughts, and your own conclusions about a subject (unless you reference the material).
- Writing up your own results obtained through lab or field experiments.
- Using your own artwork, digital photographs, video, audio, etc.
- Using "common knowledge," which is a general understanding clearly stated within a given society to reference knowledge, such as things like folklore, observations, myths, urban legends, historical events (but **not** historical documents), and common sense (be careful with this, as everyone does not come from the same background).
- Using generally accepted facts, for example, pollution is bad for the environment, and including facts that are accepted within particular discourse communities, for example, in the field of English composition studies, "writing is a process," which is a generally accepted fact.

Discussion

(May or may not be started in class)

Summary – Put It into Practice

As you have attended classes and reread the lectures, it is time to put these skills into practice and develop some concepts. Beginning with a few of the readings chosen in class, all of them have several key points within the readings. In the discussion board, we are going to practice a summary paragraph. This will be good practice for you as later you will write a summary essay. Remember, a summary is always based on the facts from the reading, and the writer presents an overview of main ideas, key points, and details with the assumption the person reading the summary has little to no background knowledge of the topic.

In brief, the summary should include the title of the work, author's name, and page number references so that the reader could easily validate information. In addition, as you summarize your work, please make sure to include at least one quote and one paraphrase from the readings to support your interpretation. For example, Bartholomae (1986) emphasizes that a student must learn to write with a variety of voices in variation of schemas to appropriately fit with the various discourses found in a collegiate community (p. 4). This is an example of a paraphrase, simply put, I used my words, but referenced the author and their work; therefore, to eliminate plagiarism using APA format, I needed to use each citation correctly within the text, placing the writing sample with an in-text citation. Remember, you must give credit, as the words, thoughts, ideas, and patterns are not your own.

Summary

A summary is a paragraph or two that will reflect solely on the main idea, or claim specified in the reading, article, or "multigenre" piece of literary composition; always cite the title and the author or authors. Moreover, a summary is rewritten into your own wording to express your interpretation of the "main idea"; however, if you reiterate the "central theme" based on the "author's" perspective, utilize statistical information, recreate an idea based as if you "were there," or any other knowledge, which "will not be considered" common fact or knowledge. Additionally, as the "writer," you should be thoughtful, positive, creative, and even logical in your approach, as you evaluate, critique, analyze, comment on, or review another; you should produce relevance, credibility, and reliability to your writing sample. Regardless, you must use in-text citations to give credit to the source or sources as you must give "credit where credit is due."

Consequently, information to keep in mind as you are creating your summary: first, be effective; as you produce effectiveness, you will reinforce basic reading strategies, such as identifying common themes or ideas (denotation, connotation), reading critically (inductive and/or deductive logic), and comprehension. Secondly, as you change the wording, "do not change" the author's original intention, or interpretation of material presented to the reader, whereas misinterpretation will create a lack of understanding of the original piece. Importantly, all academic work unless otherwise specified will remove your opinion from the interpretations; therefore, writing samples are based solely on interpretation of the reader and supported with "facts," which must contain proper in-text citation.

Finally, all writing samples should be in "third person," leave "I" out of it, as you are very important; "I" should not be the "center" or "focus" of the summary. Lastly, the summary should be based only on the information presented to the reader. "Your background knowledge" will be used for other literary interpretations; therefore, "stick to the piece"; consequently, the summary length should consist of a shortened version, not ever longer than the original work or source. Following these strategies and guidelines (tips) in several ways will help produce an effective writer.

Initial Post: Summarizing, Quoting, and Paraphrasing a Text

Initial post (150–200 words based on your perspective of one of the given readings): Remember to reread your work before you post it into the discussion board. This will be similar to your opening paragraph, which will be found in your rough draft.

The purpose of this assignment is to practice summarizing, quoting, and paraphrasing a text. Please be sure to read the piece chosen to answer the following prompts in your prewrite assignment. Remember, please only pick one prompt.

Read: Then, write a paragraph that summarizes one interesting or important idea in the text. You may write your summary in response to any one of the prompts listed below or you may focus instead on something else that interests you. **Remember:** when you write a summary, set aside your personal views and responses. Instead, focus only on explaining the ideas based on the text itself. Remember, you must stick to the facts and give credit to the source with in-text citations to eliminate plagiarism.

1. Throughout the article, does the author call the reader's attention to different bodies of evidence that either support or do not support the concept of pop culture? Summarize one of these bodies of evidence, making sure to discuss the use within the text, using at least one quotation and at least one paraphrase with proper in-text citation.
2. Does the title of this article ask a question: What are the views in this article? Further, describe how the author either does or does not answer this question throughout the course of the article. Use at least one quotation and at least one paraphrase with proper in-text citation.
3. Finally, by using summary, quotation, and paraphrasing, describe how you agree or disagree with the notion from the student essay of "mainstream" and the assumption or just a vague notion that society may assimilate everyone, but are we part of an Ancient Roman Society?

Secondary posts (100 words each for at least two or more peers or classmates in the discussion board): For the secondary post, please critique, analyze, review, and comment on your peer to see if the main point of their argument is clearly understood in the writing sample. If you agree with your peer, please state why you agree; consequently, if you disagree, please state why.

Possible questions to consider:

1. Do you have a similar view toward culture? Why? or Why not?
2. Did your classmate's post answer the question of pop culture?
3. If you agreed with your peer, did they provide support within their paragraph? Did you restate their position and extend it with facts you found?
4. Did you use proper in-text citations to support your work?

Assessment and Grading

Upload work to the appropriate area**

Writing Requirements (APA format)

- 1–2 paragraphs (approx. 250–300 words)
- 1-inch margins
- Double spaced
- 12-point Times New Roman font
- Due date: Friday before 11:59 p.m.

**Grading is 0% no submission or is 10% submission (10 points) – correct criterion will earn 10 points

As a Reminder – Academic Paragraphs

Overview

In general, academic paragraphs consist of a topic sentence, supporting evidence, and good reasons that explain why the evidence is valid and why the evidence supports the topic sentence. For this assignment, focus on developing the evidence that supports your topic sentence or the main idea that your paragraph works to discuss. Use language that appeals to our five senses of sight, sound, taste, touch, and smell. Choose specific phrases like "the tree's broad branches filled the sky" rather than general phrases like "the big tree filled the sky." Be thorough in your description by explaining your examples inasmuch detail as possible. As you begin to write, try to answer most if not all of these questions in your revision. Who? What? When? Where? Why? How? By developing a well-rounded perspective, you will help prevent your reader's confusion. Remember: never assume that the reader understands the examples and ideas that you want to discuss in the same way that you understand them.

Furthermore, paragraphs are the meat and potatoes of larger texts. They work to narrow the discussion down to bite-sized chunks of arguments. Ideally, a paragraph will contain a claim (topic sentence), evidence (details, facts, examples), and reasons why the evidence is valid and supports the major claim of the paragraph. Sometimes, writers will separate examples into their own paragraph, especially when the example is complicated or requires a lot of detail to be effective. Finally, because paragraphs are connected chunks of text that work to make a bigger argument (that is usually your thesis), it is important to think about how you transition from one paragraph to the next. Oftentimes, the transitional phrase will be at the end of the paragraph, though sometimes it will be more effective to place the transition at the start of the next paragraph.

Thus, there are two reasons for grouping sentences into a single paragraph. The first reason is to make and support an important point. Each paragraph should be focused on one main idea; when too many ideas start to crowd the paragraph, it becomes difficult for readers to keep all of the new information in their heads. Thus, writers often will break paragraphs when they shift to a new point.

The second reason that writers break up their paragraphs is to make the discussion more manageable for readers. Generally speaking, a paragraph should not be longer than about 2/3 of a double-spaced page. If your paragraphs go much longer than that, then you risk losing the attention of your reader. A good rule of thumb for an academic paragraph, especially for students who are in the early stages of their program, is to keep the paragraph limited to about 10 to 12 sentences. While many paragraphs will be much shorter than 10 to 12 sentences, you should avoid going longer than this limit.

Topic Sentences

Topic sentences state the major claim being discussed in a given paragraph. Each topic sentence consists of a word or phrase that indicates the topic and a phrase that expresses the controlling idea related to that topic. For example, the claim that "slippery floors are dangerous" consists of a topic (slippery floors) and a controlling idea related to that topic (they are dangerous). In a paragraph, this topic sentence would be followed by supporting details that illustrate how or why slippery floors are, in fact, dangerous.

It is important to distinguish between making an argument (which is what a topic sentence does) and making an announcement about what you are going to talk about within that argument. Often students will write a sentence like the following: "In this paragraph, I am going to talk about gangsta rap." While this may seem to be a topic sentence, it is actually just an announcement of the topic. In contrast, a topic sentence would add a controlling idea to the topic. For example, each of the following sentences is an argument and could serve as a topic sentence:

- Gangsta rap promotes violence in our youth.
- Gangsta rap leads to the commercialization of hip-hop.
- Gangsta rap glorifies drug culture.

Evidence

Following your topic sentence, and lying at the heart of your paragraph, is the evidence that you use to support and justify your argument. Evidence can include any examples, facts, statistics, quotations, illustrations, graphs, charts, or other details that demonstrate your point. For instance, in a paragraph arguing that gangsta rap glorifies drug culture, you might cite lyrics from Snoop Dogg's "Gin and Juice." Alternatively, you might point to Big Sean's video "A$$," which reduces women to sexual objects, to argue that rap videos objectify women. Whatever evidence you choose to use, always consider your audience and how much they know about the evidence. In order to be effective, you will have to provide enough background information for the reader to understand both your argument and how your evidence illustrates your point.

Your evidence will offer the strongest support for your topic sentence when it is specific. There are several steps that you can take to make your evidence more specific:

- Use examples that answer questions like who, what, when, where, etc.
- Use specific nouns instead of general nouns. For example, the word "dog" is a general word that refers to all sorts of animals; "Labrador Retriever" is more specific because it narrows the general category of "dogs" to one particular breed. "The old yellow Labrador Retriever lying in the doorway" is more precise than the other two because it adds concrete detail: the dog is old, yellow, and lying in the doorway.
- Use words that appeal to the senses (sight, sound, smell, taste, and touch) to create concrete images: instead of "rain," say "cold rain"; instead of "fruit," say "bitter fruit"; instead of "roses," say "sweet rose fragrance"; instead of "noisy," say "clamor"; instead of "bright," say "sunny."

- Use strong, active verbs. For example, "to walk" means to move around by using one's feet. However, there are a number of other more vigorous verbs to choose from: saunter, stroll, dash, sneak, creep, and jaunt.

Revising Paragraphs

As you revise paragraphs, consider how well the ideas in your paragraph are connected. You can make your paragraph more coherent by explaining to your reader how the pieces are connected to each other. Try using a chronological order if the ideas have a time relationship, or emphatic order if organizing the ideas from most to least important. Finally, you may also use a spatial order if you are talking about objects that have a specific relationship to each other within a particular space.

Things Needed in Academics: How to Write a Basic Essay and Read Your Essay Effectively

Basic Writing

As we begin our academic journey, several courses will expect us to write. Typically, the instructor will have us submit a "basic essay." However, if you have never written one, the process could be overwhelming. For practice, we are going to write our first essay, and it will be basic. Many courses will not allow the time for multiple drafts of a piece to be submitted, and so you will submit the final draft. After a while, the process will become easier, as you will have many opportunities to submit both rough drafts and final drafts for our course.

For the assignment, please choose a topic you are familiar and please send an e-mail with your choice to the instructor. The instructor should respond within 24 hours to confirm your idea. Remember, try not to make the topic too broad; however, you do not want to limit your topic, whereas it becomes too narrow. Over time, the process should become almost systematic as we learn to make our words count. Especially, as you will be the expert on the topic, we will need as much background within the writing sample to understand your perspective, intention, and overall purpose for us reading your work.

Begin the Research

Read/review the following search engines for finding resources for this activity:

Google

Dogpile

Blackle

Yahoo

Explorer

YouTube

- Pick a topic (must be approved)
- Research your topic (use in-text citations)
- Develop basic five-paragraph essay (thoroughly developed with academic standards)
- No rough draft should ever be a final draft
- Finished product means final draft
- Try to use at least two different search engines
- Submit outline
- Develop thesis statement

Format of Organization: Five-Paragraph Essay

The title page is the first page and includes the class name and number, title of paper, author, and date. Depending on the writing format, a title page may not have a page number and will not be counted in the total pages required.

The introduction (opening paragraph) outlines the purpose or topic of the paper, and the introduction should be considered a brief, concise paragraph or two that summarizes the content of the paper.

The body (the next three supporting paragraphs) is the main section of the paper and includes information based on paragraphs. Remember paragraphs should have one main idea that is in direct support of the thesis statement. Within each body paragraph, there will be a topic sentence (main idea of the paragraph) and supporting idea.

The conclusion or summary (final paragraph) is the portion of the paper where you will offer concluding or summarizing comments. This portion of the paper is a review and tells the reader the outcome of the paper.

The reference page is the last "stand-alone" page that will have only the references listed in alphabetical order in a hanging indent format. This page will not be counted in the final page count. Please make sure to reference the APA format. There is a difference in every academic style of writing.

Making an Essay Worth Reading, Once You Have Your Five Completed, Begin Revision

Transforming your first draft into a final draft can be a challenging process. The following questions may guide you as you decide "what and the how" to revise the essay.

Questions to Ask Yourself

The Introduction (The Open)

1. Do I catch the reader's interest, provide relevant background, and narrow the topic into a thesis sentence? Does the thesis encompass all of my key ideas? Can I underline the thesis to make sure that it is clearly stated? Do I need to adjust the thesis – either broaden or narrow it?

The Discussion (The Body)

2. Have I clearly organized my paragraphs, using one main idea per paragraph? Have I included a topic sentence to introduce the main idea for each paragraph? Do I need to adjust any topic sentences in any way?
3. Have I used transitions as links back to the thesis and to preceding paragraphs?
4. Does my argument:
    *   have a clear structure? (Can I easily outline it? Could someone else create the same outline? Does it match my original outline?)
    *   develop in the most logical order?
    *   need different organizations to be more effective?
    *   respond in sufficient depth to all aspects of the assignment?
5. Do I have enough evidence or too much? Does my evidence advance the argument in some way, without repeating the same points? Does each subargument have enough explanation and support (quotations, paraphrases, detailed discussion of events, or language of a time period)?
6. Do I explain in my own words the significance of all quotations? Am I using quotations to support my own analysis? Am I using the documentation method my professor requires?

The Conclusion (The Strong Close)

7. Does my conclusion end my thoughts and end the essay? Does it tie the paragraph together in such a way that the reader knows my purpose in writing this paper? Does it accomplish more, such as provide a broader context for the topic, propose a course of action, offer a new perspective on the topic, or end with an interesting twist? Do I leave my reader with something to ponder?

Start Those Edits: Sentence-Level Revision

8. What grammatical and stylistic concerns do I see? Have I written with clarity and conciseness?

Check for the following:

- correct word choice, punctuation, spelling, diction
- clear pronoun reference
- (tip: avoid "this is," "it is," "there is," "there are," and "that is" constructions)
- pronoun–antecedent (must match in tense and numbers [singular/plural])
- consistent verb tense
- subject–verb agreement
- variety in sentence structure

9. Is the emotional tone I use appropriate for my audience and topic?
10. What more could I say in the next draft? Could I strengthen my argument with further evidence, provide a broader context, or examine counterarguments?
11. What could I eliminate in the next draft? Have I used irrelevant or repetitive ideas and unnecessary quotations?

General Suggestions

- Read your draft aloud. We often hear weaknesses in writing more readily than we see them.
- Keep a reader in mind. Ask yourself, "Could someone else understand what I am saying?"
- Have someone else read your draft – a writing tutor, a friend, a roommate. It is very difficult to be objective about your own writing. Be sure to acknowledge all help you receive and make sure there is no conflict of interest if you work with someone else from the same class.

Now What? More Revision May Happen Again

Narrow or qualify your claim, concept, idea, or topic

The shape you give your project will depend on the position your thesis promises. You will want your thesis to make a distinct and provable claim, and then you will need to follow through with the appropriate support and evidence, or you risk losing validity.

Know the Differences between Topic Sentence and Thesis Statement

Thesis Statement: A thesis statement is typically the "longest single sentence" or "two juxtaposed sentences" in a paragraph and located within the first two introductory paragraphs. The statement defines the author's purpose or intentionality and sets the tone or dictates the overall perspective, ideals, or arguable points presented in the writing sample. The "sample," whereas, will have the details, which are purposeful, limited, or presented as an indication to the reader with more to come throughout the essay. Finally, the statement unifies the paper so that everything presented within the writing sample will have a strong point of reference. Furthermore, a good thesis statement will present the reader "with everything they will need to learn, discover, or explore about a topic."

Topic Sentence: A topic sentence is a sentence that contains the "main idea or topic" of the paper, essay, or paragraph. Particularly, only one topic per paragraph is focused on "at one time." The topic sentence may be placed in the first sentence, last sentence, the first and last sentence, or any sentence in-between (middle) to make the reader have a "clear understanding" of the idea within the paragraph. Furthermore, the topic sentence improves the essay and creates unification with proper transitional words or phrases to connect one topic to the next topic covered through the "author's interpretation." The author or writer used their knowledge, ideals, imagination, relevance, or point of view are juxtaposed, consequently, in turn, a purpose, engagement, reaction, or response, which the reader interprets the mood of the piece, and a connection to the thesis statement.

Tips for Maintaining Focus

Make a brief outline as you read your draft, underlining or summarizing in the margin the main idea of each section. Use subheadings. Even if subheadings are not retained in the final draft, they can be helpful in organizing an argument. Use phrases and sentences that work in an essay (transitions), and link those ideas together. The reader will develop stronger comprehension of your intentionality.

The Final Step

Once you have completed the final revision, it is time for one more effort – spellcheck, read aloud, read your work backward, and proofread.

You wrote it; take pride in your efforts. PROOFREAD!

Assignment – Research Essay – Educational Autobiography

Research Your Name

How do you get started drafting a research paper?

In many cases, you will find yourself refining and narrowing the scope of your research project through-out the writing process, as you develop a structure that reinforces clear, though not necessarily simple, points. Your job is to create a framework that will make your project an effective response to the original assignment. This assignment will be started in class.

Assignment – Twofold (Two Parts)

First:

Research of Your Name

For example, Mosher's (2012) "Easily Pronounced Names May Make People More Likeable" takes the approach unless you have a name "people like, you may not be liked ever." Could this be true?

For this assignment, you will research your name. Based on your reading, you will either agree or disagree with Mosher (2012), support your findings with one outside source, and support your position with at least two quotes and two paraphrases from each of the readings with proper APA format of in-text citations (Mosher, 2012, pp. 49–53). As you researched your name, were you found to be more likable, or less likable? Does this factor have an impact on your social surroundings through work, college, and home? I would argue that it does affect several aspects of "how you see yourself."

Second:

For the Educational Autobiography Portion

Writing an educational autobiography: we have the ability to connect to ourselves on many levels and to reflect on our personal experiences to the social, political, or cultural meaning of education. This assign-ment is meant to provide a guide of your **educational experiences** throughout your lifetime. The issue will not be if you are a good storyteller; the challenge will be if you are able to tell the story of your life and base it on actual social issues in education.

As a point of reference, please try to remember any "autobiographies" you may have read. Keep in mind, the person referenced, typically around their experiences in life, wrote the autobiography. For instance, the "Diary of Anne Frank," is often regarded as an autobiography. An educational autobiog-raphy will be a reflection on your personal educational events and link them to a larger social context. For example, we would share an educational event that left an impact on your life in a profound and meaningful way, such as becoming the "first-generation college student" and being an athlete created a life-changing experience.

In "Inventing the University," Bartholomae (1986) claims students have to learn the language of the university. Reflect on your "inventing yourself." Was there a time your "name" interfered with your success? Insider or outsider, something new must be learned, applied, and adapted to create success in goals, ideas, or new ventures. Education does not fall short of any of these expectations. Does the research of a topic meet the needs of the individual or the institution? Bartholomae (1986) claims repeatedly that students often "fake it till they make it." Nevertheless, "Every educational system is a political mainstay maintaining or of modifying the appropriation of discourse, with the knowledge and the power it carries with it" (p. 227). Has there been a time in your educational history where you witnessed or felt this could be true? For example, "Pull-Out Programs" are said to have given students advantages, but some research proves otherwise.

Purpose

The idea for having us reflect is to connect one of our own experiences, personal events, or social exposures, while acknowledging the educational event that had impacted our life; in fact, the more apparent the significance to the event is revealed in your writing sample, the likelihood the reader will make a personal connection to your writing sample. Remember, as you write, keep in mind the audience, because each of us comes from an eclectic array of diversity; it is easy to create bias in writing. A good way to keep this purposely organized is the use of chronological order or time order as the event unfolds.

Criteria

Things to consider: Is it a good story? Does the story have relevant meaning to education? Do you connect to a big picture? Does it make a connection to a social, political, or cultural issue? Does your experience explore or raise "new issues" coming or developing in our current society?

Audience

Remember anyone could become the reader, and there is a possibility these could lead to your first "peer review." As you are writing from one point of view, it is easy to create bias. Particularly, bias is a "one-sided view, which could be either negative or positive in outlook." In writing, we should at least acknowledge there is another side to the story.

How to Develop

Title: The connection of your writing sample and the title we give it should be a mirror of one another, for example, "Dogs on the Mississippi"; as you read the title, you would hope to read about dogs and something about the Mississippi River. However, as we began to read the piece, the reader discovers "Mississippi" is the name of a street in Little Rock, Arkansas. As a second misguided piece, the writer was using "slang for men" calling them dogs. As this writing sample reflects around you and your educational experience, it will be good practice to make the title as "true" to the story, as the reader should have as little interpretation of you as possible.

Narrative: In your youth, an elementary teacher would read the class stories, and the stories had "someone telling the story in the book." However, in this scenario, you are the narrator and your main purpose is more or less to "show and tell." As we write narratives, we want to include as much detail and support for the event to create a "big picture," as the use of adjectives will produce stronger images for the reader. Read the following: "Jack and Jill went up the hill," and now read "Jack, a virile young man, and his younger sibling Jill crossed the rocky terrain, as they climbed a steep never-ending hill full of brush, twigs, and large tree roots." The second sentence truly gave a clearer picture, although if you had the background knowledge for the "hill, Jack, or Jill," the image could still be different from the original intention of the author.

Remember, one of the hardest parts of this assignment will be to connect it to a social, political, or cultural issue. In addition, please make a personal connection and link it to a "bigger issue." As a suggestion, reference anything related to "pop culture" and use some of those issues to help develop your writing sample. You may have made a connection, as you were reading.

Issues to Consider

There are many, but these are just a small sample to explore: gender, private education, public education, socioeconomic standing, family life, extended family, sports, rote learning, authentic learning, boredom, engagement, and friendships.

Connections

In academic writing, it is important to make as many connections to the ideas of others and use their knowledge to help support your own perspective. Once you have generated a core event and put it into a narrative, identify the "conceptual pattern that links it to a larger social context." Integrate the reading, because this will help develop the "analytical aspect" of the assignment. Remember, it is one thing to "tell a story" and another to show the reader the context in a theoretical perspective, as to see it as a "bigger" piece of your life. Lastly, you have to convince the reader; yes, this event changed my life, and if I did not make the difference in my life, who or what would?

Conclusion

As we conclude our thoughts, the writing sample should show a final connection to the opening paragraph, the support in the middle, and finally the end that should match throughout your work. Your final thought must leave the reader with very little thought to your original intention of the work. In addition, as you conclude your final words and your argument, the reader's interpretation should match your point of view, even if they disagree with your position on a topic.

Remember, as you transition into your final thoughts, try to eliminate the words, "in conclusion, my conclusion, in my conclusion," whereas these are known to the reader as it is the end of your thoughts, and typically the last two paragraphs; therefore, you should have a conclusion. The use of transitional words, such as finally, particularly, lastly, furthermore, and at last, will give the reader clues that you are about to end your writing sample.

Assessment and Grading

Writing Requirements (APA format)

- 1–3 pages (approx. 300 words per page)
- 1-inch margins
- Double spaced
- 12-point Times New Roman font
- Cover page
- Reference page
- Due date: Sunday before 11:59 p.m.

**Grading is 0% no submission or is 25% submission – the correct criterion will earn 25 points.

Pick One of the Three Techniques (Do Not Do All of Them)

Drafting Arguments

More likely than not, if we think about writing, we focus on the drafting phrase. Drafting is the process of cobbling your ideas together in sentences and paragraphs. The aim of the drafting phase is to develop something that looks like a full text, though that text is usually not ready for submission when it is first completed. Drafting is usually not a one-time shot in which a student sits down for an hour or two and busts out a full-fledged essay of three to four pages! Instead, like most everything else related to writing, it is a process of its own. Successful students work in lots of revision as they draft – students may write a sentence or paragraph, then immediately revise it, or write a section of the essay, then come back later to make changes in the organization, development, etc. Drafting is thus a rather intense phase that requires lots of sustained attention and larger blocks of time.

Therefore, make it worth thinking about the situations in which you write. Consider, for example, these questions: Think about the last essay that you wrote. Where did you write it? At home? In the library? At a coffee shop? At work? Where were you sitting, and what was going on around you? Were your kids fighting over some toy in the next room? Was the TV on? Were you listening to music? What time of day was it? Early in the morning, in the afternoon, or late at night after work was finished? How did you feel? Were you tired from work or taking care of the kids? Did you just finish preparing dinner and cleaning up? Were you tired from working the night before, or were you fresh from a good night's rest?

Whatever your circumstances are, it is worthwhile to be aware of your usual practices and to make any changes in the conditions in which you work. Ideally, you should try to write when your body and mind are fresh – for most people, this happens early in the morning. Try to set aside chunks of time to work on your essay. Set clear goals for yourself as a writer for each writing session. Do your best to build in enough time to reread, revise, and edit your writing before the due date!

Rhetorical Situation

The rhetorical situation refers to the relationship between varieties of forces that affect any given text. Understanding the rhetorical situation of the text you are writing can help you make better choices related to the kinds of language, examples, and arguments that you use in your essay. Consider, for example, the kinds of language you would use on Facebook compared to the kinds of language you would use on a résumé. Think about how you would argue that you deserve a raise to your boss compared to how you would argue that you deserve a raise to a close friend, on the other hand. Paying attention to the rhetorical situation can help us understand the complex relationships between the reader, writer, text, and message.

The components of a rhetorical situation include the **text** (content, words, images, form, media), the **reader** (who brings knowledge, experience, memories, predictions, feelings, and desires to the act of reading), the **writer** (who also brings knowledge, experience, memories, feelings, intentions, purposes, and desires to the act of writing), and a **context** (which includes textual, immediate, historical, and social factors). Rhetoric is the art of understanding textual events by considering its rhetorical situation.

Simple Paragraph

At the paragraph level, we develop arguments by using a topic sentence that is supported by evidence. In general, most paragraphs in academic writing are organized by the purpose of establishing a small part of a larger argument. Often, such paragraphs will be organized by a topic sentence that makes a **claim** that makes an appeal to **ethos** (emotion, appeal), **pathos** (trustworthy, believable), or **logos** (logic, reason). Most frequently, academic arguments make claims to ethos and logos. To develop and support that claim, the paragraph will provide some **evidence** that illustrates or supports the assertions made by the claim (topic sentence). Finally, the paragraph will connect the claim and evidence by providing explicit and good **reasons** that justify why the evidence is appropriate, relevant, and sufficient to establish the claim as valid. Good reasons are smaller assertions that work when they establish a link between your evidence and your claim that your audience will accept as valid and persuasive. When you look at a paragraph, the topic sentence is the biggest claim, and the good reasons that you provide to explain your evidence are smaller claims that work to help support the topic sentence and will develop a solid thesis statement.

Revise Your Work and Test Your Organization

Organizing a sizable paper or project is rarely an easy job. For the draft of a long paper, you may want to check the structure using a method such as the following:

- **Underline the topic idea, or thesis, in your draft.** It should be clearly stated somewhere in the first few paragraphs.
- **Underline just the first sentence in each subsequent paragraph.** If the first sentence is short or closely tied to the second, underline the first two sentences.
- **Read the underlined sentences straight through as if they formed an essay in themselves.** Ask whether each sentence advances or explains the main point or thesis statement. If the sentences – taken together – read coherently, chances are the paper is well organized.
- **If the underlined sentences do not make sense, examine whether the paragraphs are clearly related to the topic.** If the ideas there really do not develop your thesis in some way, delete the whole paragraph. If the ideas are related, consider how to revise the paragraph to make the connection clearer to readers.
- **Test your conclusion against your introduction.** Sometimes the conclusions of essays contradict their opening paragraphs because of changes that occurred as the paper developed. Revise as necessary and make it often.

Another Look at the Topic Sentence versus Thesis Statement

Thesis Statement: A thesis statement is typically the "longest single sentence" or "two juxtaposed sentences" in a paragraph and located within the first two introductory paragraphs. The statement defines the author's purpose or intentionality and sets the tone or dictates the overall perspective, ideals, or arguable points presented in the writing sample, whereas the "sample" will have the details, which are purposeful, limited, or presented as an indication to the reader with more to come throughout the essay. Finally, the statement unifies the paper so that everything presented within the writing sample will have a strong point of reference. Furthermore, a good thesis statement will present the readers "with everything they will need to learn, discover, or explore about a topic."

Topic Sentence: A topic sentence is a sentence that contains the "main idea or topic" of the paper, essay, or paragraph. Particularly, only one topic per paragraph is focused on "at one time." The topic sentence may be placed in the first sentence, last sentence, the first and last sentence, or any sentence in-between (middle) to make the reader have a "clear understanding" of the idea within the paragraph. Furthermore, the topic sentence improves the essay and creates unification with proper transitional words or phrases to connect one topic to the next covered through the "author's interpretation." The author or writer uses their knowledge, ideals, as well as ideas, imagination, relevance or the point of view become juxtaposed; consequently, in turn a purpose, an engagement, the reaction or a response in which a reader can interpret sets the mood of the piece and creates the connection to the thesis statement.

Chapter 3

Skills – Visual Literacy

Time Management a Visual Perspective

This week's thoughts reflect on time. Everything in college has a deadline, "timeframe," rubric, or schedules to accomplish something. Time management is a skill that will benefit you from the time you begin to "utilize time wisely." Everyone has "things to do, people to see, and places to go"; however, as you are now planning your future, the guidance of your parents is at a distance. Your ability to manage time wisely must come first in your daily, weekly, monthly, and even yearly schedules.

In order to help with time management, one of the best tips for planning, organizing and setting goals is to develop a master calendar. As technology is one of the most advanced tools to have with in aiding success, my suggestion would be to use a calendar on your phone, and set reminders to go off at different times, so that you will be better prepared as the deadline approaches. Remember, if you do a little each day, the overall time is not so consuming, and will free up your time to explore the other benefits that campus life does hold for students.

For example:

MW – Physics project due in 2 weeks (first reminder, 3 days from input – begin project; second reminder, 3 days later – review project, and put finishing touches; third reminder, 4 days later – project due in 2 days).

Furthermore, on the master schedule you will place everything from daily routine to appointments, travel time to and from class, time spent in class, due dates, exams, mid-terms, holidays, breaks, group projects, labs, essays, papers, projects, assignments, material to read, and most important time to take breaks. As scheduling, "downtime" can be just as beneficial as you need your mind to absorb knowledge, rest, and recharge for the next assignment, task, or great adventure in a book.

Suggestions listed below as well as the events and routines you may want to include:

1. **Develop a calendar of important dates for your classes:** Tests, papers, projects, readings, mid-term and final exams, holidays, breaks, study days, etc.
2. **Enter important dates for your work, social, and family life:** Remember to include lunch…you will thank you later
3. **Each week develop a daily schedule:** That includes routines, travel time, study times, and important dates
4. **Post this schedule in your study area:** For referral and review and to mark your progress
5. **Each evening develop a schedule to help you organize the next day:** Include routines, errands, routes, time of travel, and important appointments
6. **Review each day's schedule that morning:** Be prepared just in case for that "Oh, no!" – it might be too late, but maybe not
7. **Remember to cross-off completed tasks:** This will help give you the sense of completion and double check items still not complete

Discussion 1

For this week, our topics are quite different from "vampires" to "advertising." For example, "Why Vampires Never Die" (Del Toro and Hogan, 2009, pp. 378–383), or "Art or Puffery? A Defense of Advertising" (Fletcher, 2008, pp. 114–119). As both authors create an opinion of their topic, please make sure you review your view of either for or against the main idea. Please remember to support your thoughts. As you begin to write your critique essay, you will review one of these pieces, but remember you must, if your opinion matches theirs, have one resource that matches your view to support your opinion.

For the discussion, this will be similar to your prewrite, as you will be presenting in a paragraph your thoughts based on the readings. Please remember to include the thesis statement, topic sentences, and all supporting information that will give your reader a clear picture of your interpretation. For example, Del Toro and Hogan (2009) believed that society either saw vampires as the "undead" or a "romantic" notion that people could not be without in life (p. 378). Although a vast majority may view vampires in these two categories, some people may see more as the evil creature that emerges from death itself (p.379). Immortality is not a way of life.

Initial Post

150–200 words based on your perspective of one of the given readings. Remember to re-read your work before you post it into the discussion board. This will be similar to your opening paragraph, which will be found in your rough draft.

Secondary Posts

100 words each for at least two or more peers or classmates in the discussion board. For the secondary post, please critique your peer to see if the main point of their argument is clearly understood in the writing sample. If you agree with your peer, please state why you agree; consequently, if you disagree please state why.

Sample Format

Bob, I understand that you feel vampires should be removed from our society, and you stated, "The un-dead should be buried, and left there for all eternity." However, society has a different view from yours, as some people have an everlasting devotion to someone they love, and immortality would be the only "way" these two people could be together forever.

Find a Way to Argue

Things to Consider from a Global Perspective

To make your evidence effective, explain "why" it is credible, and "why" it supports your larger claim through a series of good reasons.

To find good reasons that explain your main argument, you can use one of the following strategies:

- **Counter Argue and Reject their Claim:** A highly effective strategy is to acknowledge the counter arguments to your position, and give reasons your argument is better. For instance, "While many people say that tuition is high, the value of the education you receive is not easily quantified."
- **Give the Actual Definition to Argue:** Can you frame something in terms of another thing? A definition argument uses the pattern to draw connections between two seemingly disparate concepts. For example, "We should ban the death penalty because capital punishment is murder" argues that capital punishment is like murder. This approach is effective because while your audience may not necessarily agree with you that capital punishment should be banned, they will be ready to agree with you that murder is bad for a society, and that anything like murder is probably not good, and should therefore be made illegal.
- **Give Value or Cost to the Argument:** Say that something is a good or bad something else. An evaluative argument uses the pattern to express a judgment of value about something. For example, the argument that "Eating out three times a week is a bad way to cut down on your food budget" rejects "eating out" as an expensive practice.
- **Go Ahead, Argue it, Compare, and Contrast:** Help your readers clarify multiple sides by comparing or contrasting the objects of analysis. To express a comparison or contrast, use this pattern. For example, "Burger King Shakes are unlike McDonalds Shakes because they are creamier."
- **Oh No! Consequences of Argument:** Often, an effective way to persuade your readers is to show that certain *bad things* will happen, or certain *good things* will not happen as a result of something else. For instance, "If we shut down the government, millions of poor children will lose access to the healthcare they depend on, which could result in premature loss."

Assessment and Grading

Writing Requirements

- Initial post length: 150–200 words – Due by Tuesday at 11:59 p.m.
- Secondary post length: Minimum of 100 words per post (respond to at least two classmates) – Due by Sunday at 11:59 p.m.

**Grading is 0% if no submission, or 5% for submission (5 points) – correct criterion will earn 5 points

Building Vocabulary

In general, the greatest achievement anyone could have would be the ability to understand language. Therefore, we are building an on-going vocabulary to help enhance your success as a reader as well as a writer. Concurrently, a list of words has been provided to you, and your understanding of the meaning, both within the text and out of text, will provide a well-rounded view of language.

Please take time throughout the semester to look up these words in a dictionary and use them in your writing samples for practice. Remember to use the word and definition that will best match the context of your sentence. These words will help establish the vocabulary skills most associated with higher education. In the chapters to follow, the requirement to submit 250 words as an assignment will become part of your graded work and these words may just help.

Basic Vocabulary

access – acquire – affirm – allot – appease – assessment – attain – avid - baffle - beneficial – benefactor – bliss – clarify – clarity – collate – colleague – compatible - confidential – congenial – constraint – connotation- contention – converge – cooperate - dapper– delve – depletion – derive – denotation- detract – diligent – disarray – dismal – efficient – elaborate- elusive – empathize – empower – envision – explicit- exude – factor – faculty – fluke - formulate – fray – generate – genuine – gullible– hectic – hone – hypothesis – immerse – impartial – impassive – implausible – implicit- impress – inaccurate – incentive - inevitable – initiative – inquisitive – inscribe – intercede – interpret – irrational – jeopardize – jubilant – juxtapose – kale – keen – key – laborious – lament – lavish -liberal – malady – malevolent – management – maneuver – manipulative – manuscript – methodical – moderation – naïve – networking – nimble – omnipotent - omnipresent – opportune – opposition – option – orientation – overextend – perspective – philosophy – precarious – preclude – predicament – preliminary - prioritize – procrastinate – proficient – quality – quandary – quantity – query – rapport – reflect – reluctant – remiss – reputable – resolve – retrospect – revive - sedentary – speculate - statuesque – stimulate – surmise – sustainable – synchronize - tangible – tenacious – tenuous – tenure – thwart – trend – uncertain – unprecedented - vacate – verify – vie – visible – visionary – vital – ward – waver – weary – wise.

Concept Card

A concept card similar to a "flash card" is very useful in retrieving information. However, the main difference between the two techniques would be a concept card helps to learn the material with multiple exposures, and the "flash card" helps you to memorize. These are two completely different skills, and each has their place in academics. Nevertheless, in order to be successful, you must learn.

Template

Keep in mind, most disciplines require an extensive use of language and vocabulary. Therefore, the more practice you have using them, the better your skill will become in using this tool to learn. Remember, you need many exposures, and many educators recommend 10 exposures to any topic, before it becomes learned.

1.) WORD

3.) "PERSONAL TO YOU" – MEANING/PICTURE

FRONT

2.) DEFINITION:

4.) SENTENCE THAT MUST MATCH DEFINITION

BACK

Concept Cards

What to do…

On the front
1. Write the term in the center.
2. Write the chapter name/number and page number in the corner.
3. Include a memory device: example, sentence, rhyme, acronym, picture, etc.

On the back
1. Write a meaningful definition.
2. Write a sentence or another example with the term included.

Front	Back
Ch. 1 p.4 mortality (mort)	Def. Death rates for a population Car accidents are the number one cause of mortality for American teenagers

Front	Back
Addiction Ch. 6 p. 138 tolerance -of drugs or alcohol	Def. When progressively larger doses of a drug is needed to produce the desired effects. Quinton's tolerance to the pain medication led him to need 2 pills instead of 1 to handle the pain.

Created by Anastasia Krueck-Frahn

Template

Keep in mind, most disciplines require an extensive use of language and vocabulary. Therefore, the more practice you have using them, the better your skill will become in using this tool to learn. Remember, you need many exposures, and many educators recommend 10 exposures to any topic, before it becomes learned.

Quiz

Objective: Word usage, context meanings, recall of prior knowledge, and summary review

Part One (10 points):

Remember, knowing vocabulary opens your mind to endless possibilities…

Pick 20 words – define and use in a sentence that reflects the definition.

perspective	establish	alternative	balance	position	argument
summary	oppose	fact	opinion	annotate	culture
participation	active	context	content	solely	indivisible
quantify	pedigree	competent	correlation	delinquent	surname
peruse	cursory	glean	predetermine	caveat	revelation
copious	deluge	purport	serendipity	cohere	sporadic

Part Two (10 points):

Reflect on two readings, discussions in class, on the discussion board, or essay papers that we have written. Now write a comparative summary, please remember to include the author, title, and all relevant information for completing the summary. Length: 3–5 paragraphs

Discussion 2 – APA format: Development of Idea, Non-Sense or New Concept

The Idea, Non-Sense, New Concept is ALL YOU

(Create a brand new word for it – take two preexisting words and combine them)

For example, Writad is the ability to read and write at the same time and is an inexpensive tool.

Objective

For this week's discussion board, the initial post will be the uploading and practicing of the title page/ cover page required for APA format, and the next page, which will be the "first page of text." The first page should reflect the number 2, and the words "Running head" will be removed from the page. All sequential pages to follow will reflect the same style. The text to include on the first page of text is your opening paragraph; please include a paragraph that will be used for your Non-Sense Essay and class presentation. You need to practice catching the reader's attention and developing an awesome thesis statement that will tell the reader "everything" that you will write. This is the final step to polishing your paper in an APA style.

Initial Post (150–200 words)

Included within your first page of text will be the development of your freewriting, which you have begun in class. Keep in mind, we should now reflect a full-fledged academic paragraph, such as your opening paragraph. Focus on correct paragraph format, topic sentence, thesis statement, supporting details, grammar, mechanics, cohesion, articulation, clarity, "imagination," and most importantly, "content" that will create your "position" for the "new concept." In addition, chose to expand the original "freewrite" and place the concept with relevance to the 21st century, possibly "new craze," a must have item for every household…**be creative**.

Secondary Post (minimum of 100 words per post)

Respond to the content and development of your peers' paragraphs. Is there a strong topic sentence? Within the writing sample, does the either question of "why or why not?" come into the writers' position of the concept created for the discussion board. Does the writer provide sufficient and compelling support, descriptive details, examples, etc.? What suggestions do you have to improve the idea and/or the writing? Please remember, their "writing" needs improvement; please be positive; however, guide to a possible solution, or re-state "your favorite lines" to show a connection to their writing sample.

1. I understood your thesis statement – you said...
2. Based on your thesis statement, the title of your work does not tell me enough information you have considered using the following information?
3. The "Running head" format is correct or incorrect...and give suggestions to fix it.
4. Opening paragraph should be at least 5–7 sentences; did your peer complete this successfully? If the paragraph fell shorter than required, could you give information to help expand your peers writing sample?
5. How could you make the "informative paragraph" an argument?

How to Develop this Non-Sense

Think of something that you may have always wanted, or had an idea of, but did not know where it was, or if it even existed. Prewriting is the first step to creating your "new concept," but the paragraph posted must be an academic paragraph. Which in turn means that the paragraph must be grammatically correct, with the exception of your "new concept."

Prewriting or freewriting is a strategy used in writing that will come before the initial piece, hence the word part "pre," which means to come before; equally important to this strategy is to develop possible ideas to focus on our overall thoughts, ideas, or reflections on a given topic, concept, or reading. Try making a list of possible topics or talking about the topic with a friend, family member, or coworker. Use this prewriting strategy to come up with a set of possible terms to define in the initial post. Once you have a list, chose one that you can write about for this discussion assignment.

In other words, as you write your initial post, use freewriting techniques to develop supporting details related to your chosen topic. When you freewrite, the aim is just to put your ideas down in writing – grammar and sentence structure do not matter in a freewrite. Instead, the most important objective of freewriting is to come up with new ideas, examples, details, explanations that help "you" comprehend a better understanding of your chosen topic.

There are three important rules to help you be productive in prewriting or freewriting:

1. **Never stop writing:** Even if you feel like you have run out of things to say, just write a sentence stating the topic until new thoughts emerge. For example, you might write this statement repeatedly when freewriting about family gatherings: "What else can I say about family gatherings? What else can I say about family gatherings? What else can I say about family …"
2. **Never censor yourself:** Even if you feel like your ideas are stupid, irrelevant, unimportant, or that you cannot find the right words, just keep writing. Once you are done with the freewrite, you can go back and decide ideas to keep, and ideals to discard (which ideas are useful and which ideas are not so useful). During the course of freewriting, do not stop writing even when you cannot find the right word; you know you spelled something wrong, or you think now that your ideas do not make sense.
3. **Write for a short period of time:** It will be difficult to sustain your attention while freewriting, so set short periods of time – at first, only 5 minutes. With practice, you may be able to freewrite for 10 minutes or more.

Example of a Non-Sense Discussion Board Initial Post

Remember for this assignment, we are to invent a new word that combines two existing words in order to express a new idea. For example, look at the created word to express a new concept of "oopix."

Over time, it has been said that people are prone to make mistakes. People cannot get enough of this new gadget found in grocery stores, drug stores, office suppliers, and even toy stores, "Oopix" is the best 21st century product, as it has been created to scan over any type of paper, erase the error, and fuse ink onto the paper as you type into the prompter the missing content. This is a great system to replace any found error, especially in time constraints, and has been known to save you hours of looking for a computer and printer to redo work. It is the next must have in every household, and office alike, as you will not understand the simplification of the process, until you needed the job "done yesterday," or plainly lack the time today, supplies are limited; do not wait.

Consequently looking at the new concept, you should be able to guess the origin of the two words used to create this concept, whereas you may have guessed the combination of the words oops and fix without directly stating to the reader your new creation. Do not give the two separate words in the writing sample. This strategy allows the writer to have an idea, create circumstances for the idea, develop all content, and give meaning to a word that does not exist, in turn allows the reader the ability to see the writer's intentionality and perspective as they created their writing sample.

The reader-based concept on background knowledge should be able to develop an understanding that utilized their own point-of-view, which should match the writer's purpose and tone of the piece closely. Note if there were a misinterpretation of the writing sample, this would mean the reader and writer does not match in perspective. Nevertheless, the writer has lost the reader through nothing more than a "loss of translation," or interpretation; therefore, the writer may need to add more details, give more background information, or clues that may be needed to "paint" a more meaningful connection to a good writing sample. Remember, not all writing is directly stated; therefore, the meaning could be implied throughout the piece, but the reader should be able to understand "what you are saying."

Finally, remember that your concept can be related to technology, habits, activities, workplaces, schools, government, wildlife, etc. Once you have developed an idea use the freewrite to explore the concept, then develop it with supporting examples. Ultimately, your objective is to begin to develop a definition of your invented concept supported with specific examples.

Assessment and Grading

Writing Requirements

- Due date: Initial post: Friday by 11:59 p.m.
- Due date: Secondary posts: Sunday by 11:59 p.m.

**Grading is 0% if no submission, or is 15% submission – correct criterion will earn 15 points

Assignment – Non-sense Essay

Remember for this assignment, we are to invent a new word that combines two existing words in order to express a new idea. For example, to express a new concept of "oopix," it has been said that people are prone to make mistakes. People cannot get enough of this new gadget found in grocery stores, drug stores, office suppliers, and even toy stores. "Oopix" is the best 21st century product, as it has been created to scan over any type of paper, erase the error, and fuse ink onto the paper as you type into the prompter the missing content. This is a great system to replace any found error, especially in time constraints, and has been known to save you hours of looking for a computer and printer to re-do work. It is the next must have in every household, and office alike, as you will not understand the simplification of the process, until you needed the job "done yesterday," or plain lack the time today, supplies are limited; do not wait.

Consequently, looking at the new concept you should be able to guess the origin of the two words used to create this concept, whereas you may have guessed the combination of the words oops and fix without directly stating to the reader your new creation. This strategy allows the writer to have an idea, create circumstances for the idea, develop all content, and give meaning to a word that does not exist, in turn allows the reader the ability to see the writer's intentionality and perspective as they created their writing sample. The reader based on background knowledge should be able to develop an understanding that utilized their own point-of-view, which should match the writer's purpose and tone of the piece closely. Note if there were a misinterpretation of the writing sample. This would mean the reader and writer do not match in perspective. Nevertheless, the writer has lost the reader through nothing more than a "loss of translation," or interpretation; therefore, the writer may need to add more details, give more background information, or clues may be needed to "paint" a more meaningful connection to a good writing sample. Remember, not all writing is directly stated; therefore, the meaning could be implied throughout the piece, but the reader should be able to understand "what you are saying."

Remember, your concept can be related to technology, habits, activities, workplaces, schools, government, wildlife, etc. Once you have developed an idea use the freewrite to explore the concept, then develop it with supporting examples. Ultimately, your objective is to begin to develop a definition of your invented concept supported with specific examples.

Academic Essay – Non-sense Concept Creation (40 points)

Put it All Together – Remember the Steps

Now, as you move from the first draft through the revision and editing process to the final draft, focus first on big picture issues or global perspective. Does your essay make a point (argument) about the term you have coined? Do you support that point (argument) with specific details (evidence)? Have you organized your essay in a way that makes it easy for someone who has not spent nearly as much time working on his (thinking, reading, and writing) as you have? As stated, these basic questions are some that all writers must wrestle with, as they revise their texts. Use the feedback you received from your peers, instructor, tutors, and friends as you move forward, as the "non-sense word or new concept was part of our discussion boards."

Next, after you have fully addressed these issues to the best of your ability, look at your writing from the smaller issues or a linear perspective. Focus on the sentence-level issues like sentence structure, punctuation, and spelling. Try to make your draft as clean as possible before you turn it in. To uncover sentence-level errors, try reading your paper out-loud, or aloud; ask a friend to read the draft and circle any sentences that seem awkward; use grammar-check functions; talk with a tutor or your instructor about the paper. Remember, this is the process of writing, and your review will give you the best writing sample. Once you feel like everything is polished, turn in your final draft.

Description

An academic essay consists of three main sections: Introduction, body, and conclusion. Whereas, many of us have heard of the five-paragraph essay, an **introduction** catches the reader's attention, introduces the topic, and gives the thesis statement. Next, the **body** consists of three paragraphs that develop or explain the argument expressed in the thesis statement through topic sentences, supporting examples/evidence, and good reasons for the **conclusion** closure to the argument by explaining why the argument is important, or by discussing the implications of the argument.

Remember, the next step is to revise this assignment, draw on what you learned in other or previous coursework, develop paragraphs that are organized around a topic sentence that states one main idea, and are supported by sufficient, descriptive examples that illustrate your point. As you develop the discussion posts into an essay, focus on the connections between paragraphs. In addition, for this first essay assignment, work to develop a strong introduction as you capture the reader, an effective and well-organized body, and an interesting conclusion with a twist of the thesis statement for more dynamics.

Assignment

Write an essay that discusses the "new concept" you defined as the academic paragraph, and the rough draft assignments. In order to expand your definition, concept, or belief into a longer essay, you might want to consider one of the following strategies:

- Discuss why this new concept is important and should be used in 21st century American society.
- Explain and evaluate the implications of the concept that you have defined.
- Explore the causes and/or effects of the concept that you have defined for our society.
- Commodity in society that will create to a marketing plan or "selling pitch."
- Household need to reflect society as a whole will benefit from the enrichment of the product.

Assessment and Grading Essay

Upload Work to the Appropriate Area**

Writing Requirements (APA format)

- 2 pages (approximately 600 words)
- 1-inch margins
- Double-spaced
- 12-point Times New Roman font
- Cover page
- Reference page (as the reading is the source- please use in-text citations)
- Due Date: Sunday by 11:59 p.m.

**Grading is 0% if no submission, or 40% on submission – correct criterion will earn 40 points

Presentation Day of Class (10 points) to be Announced in Class (See Rubric)

For the actual presentation, you will "sell" your new concept in class. As you will use the following rubric for key points to do, you show your peers that your concept is just as good as the next product, next advertiser, finally, the 21st century concept. Remember, the visual aides are to give your "idea" support; this is not a power point presentation with text, but a visual representation of your overall concept. The rubric will be your best guide, so please peruse it.

Essay Grading Rubric   Professor Krueck-Frahn 100 possible points

Content and Development	Excellent	Above Average	Average	Lacks Sustenance	Inadequate	Failure to Comply
Possible 25 pts Must comply with the entire criteria	25	21	19	16	13	0

Criteria: Meets all requirements of the essay guidelines – fulfill the assignment guidelines
- Reflects adequately the main idea, provides support of text, shows originality
- Demonstrates creative or critical thought to a topic/concept
- Recognizes the reading, documentation, and author
- Eliminates bias, opinion, or hearsay within the essay
- Justifies the "topic" with proper pattern of organization
- Writes from multiple perspectives – typically third person
- Considers multiple points-of-view in the review of literature
- Adequately produces explanation, development, support with description, examples, facts

Thesis Statement	Excellent	Above Average	Average	Lacks Sustenance	Inadequate	Failure to Comply
Possible 10 pts Must comply with the entire criteria	10	8	7	6	5	0

- Must be at least one to two sentences that states the "main idea" or "claim"
- Must show all significance to the topic, be specific, and arguable
- Must provide all relevant information in a " preview" of the entire writing sample

Structure	Excellent	Above Average	Average	Lacks Sustenance	Inadequate	Failure to Comply
Possible 25 pts Must comply with the entire criteria	25	21	19	16	13	0

- Overall produces logic (reasoning)
- Introduction and Conclusion each meet functionality (introduce and finalize)
- Each paragraph has "one topic" per paragraph; focus is a single point (unity)
- Paragraphs are coherent (flow)
- Uses transitional word/phrases effectively (connection)
- Paragraphs have a topic sentence, instead of general topic (specific)

Source and Documentation	Excellent	Above Average	Average	Lacks Sustenance	Inadequate	Failure to Comply
Possible 20 pts Must comply with the entire criteria	20	17	15	13	10	0

- – Avoid Plagiarism – use in-text citation and integrates sources for support
- – Must use assortment of quotations, paraphrases, summaries (proper citation)
- – Essay demonstrates comprehension of its sources or reference materials
- – Must have both in-text citations and Work Cited Page in proper APA format

Grammar and Mechanics	Excellent	Above Average	Average	Lacks Sustenance	Inadequate	Failure to Comply
Possible 20 pts Must comply with the entire criteria	20	17	15	13	10	0

- – Conforms to Standard American English
- – Displays correct grammar, sentence structure, punctuation, diction, etc.
- – Appropriate language – lacks jargon, cliché, colloquialism, vulgarity

Automatic Deductions	Margin or Font	Lacks Running Header	Incorrect Paragraph Format	Incorrect Assignment Length	Late	Correction to Rough Draft
Must comply with the entire criteria	5	5	5	5	10	10

Lecture 2

Visual Literacy – Use of Images/Pictures

Visual Literacy Defined

"Visual literacy is a set of abilities that enables an individual to effectively find, interpret, evaluate, use, and create images and visual media. Visual literacy skills equip a learner to understand and analyze the contextual, cultural, ethical, aesthetic, intellectual, and technical components involved in the production and use of visual materials. A visually literate individual is both a critical consumer of visual media and a competent contributor to a body of shared knowledge and culture" (Retrieved: Visual Literacy Standards, 2000).

As our 21st century develops, so does our ever-evolving way of thinking to gain information, learn knowledge, and continue our process to become a lifelong learner. Did you know that one of your "senses" could actually create enough data to secure an image, help develop a concept, and transform concrete learning into abstract thought? Our visual perception has the ability to create a long-term connection to both print as well as imagery. As we move forward into our course, the use of visuals will increase, as will our need to draw a picture, produce more details, and gain a more "global" perspective to the world around us.

The following information retrieved from the "Information Literacy Competency Standards for Higher Education" should give a clearer picture to learning, and the environment of the 21st century. "The Standards address these distinct characteristics of images and visual media and challenge students to develop a combination of abilities related to information literacy, visual communication, interpretation, and technology and digital media use." Other forms of literacy that play an intricate role with "visual literacy" would be the need for "information literacy," or simply the use of computers via technology. However, the "sharing" of the information retrieved has raised issues with "ethical and legal issues."

Particularly, on one hand, information literacy extends thoughts (understanding), promotes the "seeking" of knowledge (searching), initiates results (data), and sustains "generalizations" of information (evaluating data). On the other hand, the use of technology allows intellectual abilities "through critical discernment and reasoning which focus on content, communication, analysis, and evaluation." Actively using these tools supports a "fluency" to the literacy, and in turn begins to crystalize the visual of a lifelong learner as a connection to the bigger personal goal. Whereas, the "images" tend to serve as information, as well as supporting information, while researching in a "text-based environment." As Kodak stated, "A picture is worth a thousand words." As the closer you look "at something," the clearer the image should become, as it is through the "eye" the creativity, aesthetic, prior knowledge, and prediction will come into play. As a good exercise, look at the following images, and try not to look ahead. Ask yourself…are these images the same? Do I need more information? Have I seen these images before?

Photo courtesy of Anastasia Krueck-Frahn

If you answered these images are the same, you are correct, as only the perspective has changed to give a different angle. Now as the full picture emerges, you only see the image, remember, again that we only see it from "one perspective," mine. Did you find the original angle? She has her hands in the air.

Photo courtesy of Anastasia Krueck-Frahn

Chapter 4

Critical Thought

Think About it...How to Present?

One challenge that writers face is to learn how to be open to the constructive criticism offered by others. To support this development, the goal of the class is to create a sense of community in which we feel comfortable enough to discuss openly our ideas and to comment on each other's written work. Below is a sample of the beginning to a presentation, and feedback to guide the student to writing with a stronger expression of the topic.

Student sample of the presentation a "non-sense word" or a new concept:

"Once in a while, everybody gets behind, but there are things to do. We get up, get ready, then who knows; it just happens. The amegabot will help. All you got to do is buy it. The rest is easy. Everyone will want one."

Consequently, this author presented his assignment in the mannerism of "Problem-Solution" writing format for a composition class. They stated the "problem" in several different ways within the writing sample, and demonstrated a limited understanding of the connections among key points. However, they lacked a thesis statement that could show clear articulation and focus on the topic.

Moreover, the topic sentence lacked coherence, and formatting of the "problem" and clear "solutions" given on a limited basis, demonstrating a limited understanding of topic, or relationships between key points-of-view. They integrated support for some points, but lacked sources to show evidence of content explored. The critical thinking proposed throughout the writing leaves the audience with multiple questions, and lends the piece toward a more emotional rhetoric, rather than a notable insight to a "problem."

The Day of the Presentation

All right, as some of us present, remember this is very similar to writing. Therefore, we must take a position, clearly state our objections, and present our idea with a strong conviction to the area we are trying to "sell." As we will have several presentations throughout the semester, practicing a "speech" in front of a mirror will begin to give you confidence, as you will see yourself as others will see you. The key to success in a presentation is to "know your product, topic, idea, concept, or research in a given field." Please peruse the sample of a rubric for our presentation, as the key points will be the fields in which you are graded. Consequently, presentation is everything. Hence, please look at the presentation in "What Constitutes Success?" Bessie Anderson Stanley (1904) depicted

He has achieved success who has lived well, laughed often and loved much; who has enjoyed the trust of pure women and the love of little children; who has filled his niche and accomplished his task; who has left the world better than he found it, whether by an improved poppy, a perfect poem, or a rescued soul; who has never lacked appreciation of earth's beauty or failed to express it; who has always looked for the best in others and given them the best he had; whose life was an inspiration; whose memory a benediction (Stanley, 1904).

The Presentation of Cognition (Critical Thought)

To put presentation differently, but have a very clear purpose, think of Benjamin Bloom (1956). He designed the concept of "taxonomy," which helped create a development for "higher order thinking." Later in history, one of his own students adapted the model and improved on it; therefore dividing it into two specific dimensions of knowledge and cognition. Idealistically, the overall concept reflects on metacognition (the way we think about thinking) and cognition (the way we learn).

Simply put, as we study learning the process of "how we think," we will become instrumental in "how we learn" and in our own integral role for obtaining the information necessary for your success to become a "lifelong learner." Nevertheless, our ability to reference knowledge, seek skills, and the attitude to accomplish a task will be the difference in academics, because without these adaptations it appears most things in life cease to exist.

Discussion 1

As media plays an intricate role in the life of many American's, from the use of television, newspapers, magazines, electronic media, and blogs, then comes the reliability of information being passed from one source to another. Where does the accountability to public responsibility come into play, as some people will believe just about anything? As we gather information, it has been strongly suggested that two different things a person should do before coming to a conclusion. First, make a prediction to the outcome, whereas, the titles of the piece will be a good indicator of the information that should follow throughout the text. Second, use any prior knowledge that we may have on a subject, and find more information that either opposes or substantiates and corroborates the truth.

Initial Post (150 words)

For this exercise, please recall the first time you ever heard of "Facebook, Twitter, Instagram, You Tube" and the like…now think of the first time you signed up for one of those accounts. If you have used one or more of these services over time, please include your feelings on the "media now." Has your use increased or decreased? Why do you log onto "Facebook?" Do you ever find yourself logging into Facebook and just regretting it once you have seen the theme for the day, or the dark and gloomy posts of "friends" that just appear to be going nowhere in their life. We often feel as though our "friends" would not share their "drama," because it tends to change our mood from that point of the day. We often feel accomplished as we read several "success stories." After all, these seem to be stories one could relate or better yet a story being close to one of our own, or maybe the story is the goal set for ourselves. Nevertheless, as you reflect, make sure there are examples, situations, or scenarios to support your post.

Secondary Posts (100 words each at least two or more classmates)

As you read your peers work, could you make a connection to their claim. Were you able to "put yourself in their shoes?" Please write an extension to their original work, as to add onto the actual story. Consequently, the story you are extending should be based on facts, however, the secondary posts is fictitious.

Read the following story and determine real or make believe:

Well it is Tuesday, and Jamie should be posting their thought of the day. Yep, there it is just like every other Tuesday. Jamie said, "OMG what a day, first I got stopped by a train on the way to work, then someone got a flat tire, made it to the highway, stopped on the highway semi turned over, made it to work two hours late. The boss said, no excuses you're fired. All I can say is why? The rent is due, and food needs to be bought for the kids, not to mention this could definitely ruin our relationship."

Sample of a Secondary Posts

Frank, here is your story with a twist.

Jamie said, "OMG what a day, first I got stopped by a train on the way to work, then someone got a flat tire, made it to the highway, stopped on the highway semi turned over, made it to work two hours late. The boss said, no excuses you're fired. All I can say is why? The rent is due, and food needs to be bought for the kids, not to mention this could definitely ruin our relationship." Susie came home from work and saw Jamie already home. She said, "You are home early everything okay?" Jamie said, "I don't want to talk about it." She said, "Why?" He said, "You would not believe me anyway."

Assessment and Grading

Writing Requirements

- Initial post length: 150–200 words
  - o Due by Tuesday at 11:59 p.m.
- Secondary posts length: Minimum of 100 words per post (respond to at least two classmates)
  - o Due by Sunday at 11:59 p.m.

**Grading is 0% if no submission, or 5% on submission (5 points) – correct criterion will earn 5 points

Formal Writing versus Informal Writing

Did you know that we do not speak as we write. Therefore, it could be stated, "We do not write as we speak." In particular, as we are in an academic setting, we will be called upon to write essays, short responses, use collaborative discussion boards, and present material researched for a given topic, concept, or study. Therefore, the use of colloquial language, simile, metaphors, vernacular, adages, puns, jargon, slang, and the like we use in everyday common speech, typically, are prohibited from our academic work. Nevertheless, as these types of genre have a specific use, there may be a time you might be able to use them.

Formal Writing

Formal writing has a specific purpose in academics, and will have us present material, content, findings, research, and many others based solely on a factual basis with support from outside "peer reviewed academic" research. As we write, the style becomes dictated usually from the APA format, MLA format, or CMS format, depending on the discipline, requirements of the course, and university acceptance of the text produced to represent your work. Primarily, as we will conduct research, present ideas, interpretations, and summarize readings, the use of support with proper in-text citation and reference pages must be included within our writing sample.

Informal Writing

Informal writing, on the other hand, tends to be used in academics for reflecting, recalling, understanding, completing a reading, or summarizing assignments. In addition, informal writing would be used more for a prewriting strategy versus a polished essay. One requirement of our course would be the discussion boards, even though they are primarily set in an informal setting. The use of "formal documentation within your text" will be required to show support of your interpretation, opinion, or overall emotion of any given piece. However, as we are in a diverse classroom, eliminating bias and asking questions as we write will promote positive writing samples.

Examples of Informal and Formal Writing Samples

Informal (in-text citation)	Formal (in-text citation)
• Journal	• Book/Article Review
• Book/Article Report	• Compare/Contrast Paper
• Vocabulary	• Definition Paper
• Note-taking	• Reflective Paper
• Process Reflection	• Response/Reaction Paper
• Summaries	• Research Paper
• Annotation	• Annotation

Discussion 2

Bill Bryson (1994) stated in America that we will buy anything, if we believe it to be true; hence, "The Hard Sell: Advertising in America." Where does the accountability to public responsibility come into play, as some people will believe just about anything? As we gather information, it is strongly suggested that two different things a person should do before coming to a conclusion. First, make a prediction to the outcome, whereas, the titles of the piece will be a good indicator of the information that should follow throughout the text. Second, use any prior knowledge that we may have on a subject, and find more information that either opposes or substantiates and corroborates the truth. Pop culture tends to take the "now" and make it the "must have" within our society, the jingles (earworms), slogans, and subtle hints, even subliminal throughout a given advertisement, may just "change our view."

Initial Post (150 words)

For this exercise, please recall the first time you ever heard of a jingle, slogan, or even possibly an advertisement. If you are having difficulty, and must use our current times, please look at billboards, listen to the radio, view the internet, or drive by a "fast food restaurant." Nevertheless, as you reflect make sure there are examples, situations, or scenarios to support your post. Remember to give as much background information to support your post. Try including age, time, place, or even a "year" as a point of reference, as this will help us visualize your experience. In order to make your opinion more valid, please include at least one quote and one paraphrase to support your writing sample.

Read the following for an example of creating a jingle that has stuck throughout time. "Plop, plop, fizz, fizz, oh what a relief it is...." In my youth my mom would always complain of an upset stomach, and one day, viewing the television it appeared as a commercial for "Alka-Seltzer." My mom was so excited, we left everything, literally ran to the store, and there it was on the shelf. Needless to say, we walked home. Mom followed the directions, and felt better quickly. Many years later, I still hear the jingle in my head, and if I get a sour stomach buy the product.

Secondary Posts (100 words each at least two or more classmates)

As you read your peers work, could you make a connection to their claim. Were you able to "put yourself in their shoes?" Please remember to re-state some of your peer's original post to "show a connection," and in turn extend your interpretation with similar experiences or different experiences to make an overall connection to the reading. In addition, you will need to support your interpretation, please include either a quote or paraphrase from the reading, remember all support must use proper APA in-text citations.

Assessment and Grading

Writing Requirements

- Initial post length: 150–200 words
  o Due by Friday at 11:59 p.m.
- Secondary posts length: Minimum of 100 words per post (respond to at least two classmates)
  o Due by Sunday at 11:59 p.m.

**Grading is 0% if no submission, or 10% on submission – correct criterion will earn 10 points

Assignment – Critique Essay

What is a critique? A critique is an analysis of a written text based on evidence, which is extracted from the document. A critique can also be applied to media images as well as spoken discourse; however, most university courses focus on the criticism of written works or documents, auditory assessment, or visual perception.

Initially, in assessing written works, the work itself must be understood. If the content is misunderstood, then the critique will be misapplied. In other words, the interpretation you have formulated in the reading of the piece will not match the writer's intention of the material they have presented to be read. The following suggestion is strongly recommended, please read and re-read through the piece at least twice – first for content, and then for analysis. While analyzing text mark the areas that are of significance. Whereas, the content of the information presented is to gain knowledge of topics, ideas, and specific points.

Next, underline key terms and phrases. Also, if there are areas that are unclear or confusing, those sections should be marked. Be sure to ask questions about areas that are not fully understood as these may be critical to the analysis being conducted. Once the text has been read and understood, the text, which has been analyzed, can be broken apart; consequently, a critique can be written.

Critiques serve to examine an author's claim/argument. Certain questions should be posed in the text:

- What is the author's main claim or thesis statement? If no such statement exists, what serves as the focus of the work?
- How clearly does the author present the problem or thesis statement?
- How does the author achieve the goal of the work? Does the author do so effectively? Why or why not?
- What is the particular evidence used to support the author's claim?
- How well does the author describe methods or supporting evidence?
- Does the author logically support his/her argument with an organized structure and coherent development?
- Do the sections make sense as presented? Why or why not?

Writing a Critique

Once these questions are answered, the critique can be written, analyzing the text that has been assessed. In writing a critique, both strengths and weaknesses of the argument should be acknowledged, beginning with the main claim of the specific text. After discussing the claim's efficacy, the supporting evidence should be examined for pertinence and importance. Has the supporting information been used appropriately and accurately? Each piece of "important" evidence should be addressed for strengths and weaknesses, but it is important to remember that when assessing individual pieces of evidence, each piece should be looked at individually or in one paragraph to avoid confusion in organization.

All too often, writers try to analyze a chunk of text that is too big for a short analysis paper and the important elements can become lost. Small sections of text should be assessed for a higher level of examination accuracy. So try to focus on one or two pages at a time for similar topics and ideas, versus the entire chapter or unit. Remember, it is easier to do things in small steps than trying to bypass the necessary steps to be finished.

As you write your rough draft try to focus first on big picture issues or global perspective. Does your essay make a point (argument) about the term you have coined? Do you support that point (argument) with specific details (evidence)? Have you organized your essay in a way that makes it easy for someone who has not spent nearly as much time working on this (thinking, reading, and writing) as you have? As stated, these are some of the basic questions that all writers must wrestle with, as they revise their texts. Use the feedback you received from your peers, instructor, tutors, and friends as you move forward. Please review the guidelines for writing a critique. As you read, "Why Vampires Never Die" or "Art or Puffery? A Defense in Advertising," review the key topics that will lead to the "steps" in writing a critique of literature. Please examine one or two key issues that are addressed in the piece to help you write your critique.

A brief outline of a critique is provided for you as you proofread your critique. Does my critique have the following information within my writing sample? A critique is a paper that gives a critical assessment of a book or article.

Steps to Review

- Begin by reading the book or article and annotate as you read.
- Noted the author's main point/thesis statement.
- Divide the book/article into sections of thought and write a brief summary of each thought in your own words.

Introduction

Start your critique with sentences giving the following information:

- Author's name
- Book/Article title and source
- Author's thesis statement

Summary

Summarize the author's purpose and main points/evidence cited that are used for backup.

Review and Evaluate

To critically review the piece, ask the following questions:

- ✓ What are the credentials/areas of expertise of the author?
- ✓ Did the author use appropriate methods to gather the evidence?
- ✓ Was the evidence used by the author accurate?
- ✓ Does the author's use and interpretation of this evidence lead the reader to the same conclusion?
- ✓ Did the author build a logical argument?
- ✓ Is there other evidence that would support a counter-argument?
- ✓ Are the article and the evidence still valid or are they outdated, leading to an invalid conclusion?
- ✓ Was the author successful in making his/her point?

Conclusion

Wrap up by:

- Stating whether you agree with the author (do not use the words agree or disagree).
- Backup your decisions by stating your reasons.
- Give a general opinion of the work…

Assessment and Grading

Upload Work to the Appropriate Area**

Writing Requirements (APA format)

- 2 pages (approximately 600 words)
- 1-inch margins
- Double-spaced
- 12-point Times New Roman font
- Cover page
- Reference page (as the reading is the source, please use in-text citations)
- Due date: Friday by 11:59 p.m.

**Grading is 0% if no submission, else is 45% submission – correct criterion will earn 45 points

Chapter 5

Journal Writing and Basic Writing Skills

Journal Writing Reflections versus Predictions

Journal Writing

Writing is very complicated, especially as we record information in the way we see things, so our perspective gives only one view of a larger picture and journals are a good reflective sample of writing. We will begin to look at writing journal entries in a notebook, possibly on the discussion board, and definitely, in a collaborative writing exercise within small groups throughout our classroom. The purpose of different journal entries will give an image of your perspective, your peers perspective and consensus of the topic, concept or idea being discussed in a reading, research or "cultural aspect" of the learning environment, and theoretically speaking one of the best ways to improve writing.

For our purpose, we practice reflecting on the readings, and discussions held within our classroom. As the time for you to write journal entries for our tradebook will become "second nature," the more you practice something, the more comfortable you become with the process as a whole. An interesting fact will be from the etymology of the word journal, as derived from the French word meaning "day."

Certainly, our journals will be released for publication, as the process for the assignments are the main concern. In addition, your journal will be a place for you to record your thoughts, viewpoints, and opposition to views on any given topics, concepts or subjects are being taught in the classroom. Lastly, the criterion will shift with the interests, within the community, or other focal points deliberated through multimodalities or different mediums of genre. Please reflect objectively, as to "step back" to see the larger picture. Developing a habit or establishing a pattern of "when" to record your entries is often a good idea. Idealistically, the more you practice writing in all forms, the better you will become, and in turn, the more you read different writing samples; the possibilities become endless with your ability to read, write, and think.

Predictions

Nevertheless, as we compare predictions to events, facts, or hypothetical information, we realize these are things or pieces of information that may or may not come true, materialize, or reflect the future. Whereas, the facts have presented themselves either in a deductive reason, or an inductive reason depending on the logic required to assess the situation. According to Merriam-Webster, a prediction is "a statement about what will happen or might happen in the future, or the act of saying what will happen in the future."

In general, we try to make predictions of just about everything in our life. We guess the "winning lottery numbers," make bets on the relationships our friends are in, and guess how long they will last (we may say – bet they won't last), predict the outcome of our classes before we begin them, and we should predict every piece of information that we read. As the titles, subtitles, bold print, and key phrases give "clues" to gain a deeper perspective of the reading or writing sample, a prediction for you, as all in academics will attest those that put forth the effort "to do," will have it done.

Discussion 1

Christian (2011) "The Problem with YouTube" discusses some very interesting notions of World Wide Web search engine. In fact, "YouTube" is the second largest search engine to gather information on a daily basis. As you gathered information based on the title, was your prediction correct? Did you develop good questions, before you read? As the majority of you have grown during the "information technology age," were you permitted to use "YouTube" as part of your academic search? For this discussion, please reflect to a time that you viewed a video on "YouTube." Why did you visit the site? Did you ever go back to find the same video? Have you ever been back? If you have not had the chance to view "YouTube" and need assistance, please ask a peer to help you with one of their favorites. A word of caution, please ask the peer the name of the video, and ask for a brief description before you view it.

Remember, this is a "G" rated class; therefore, the content must be viewable for all ages.

Take a look at the video…does this fall into the content that Christian (2011) spoke of in the reading? Is the site viral? Whereas, Christian (2011) stated the focus is on views, and not necessarily content or quality of the video (p. 217). Could you argue he is wrong? Why have visual perspectives at all?

"Feline" Found on YouTube

Initial Post (150–200 words)

Please locate a video on "YouTube." As you view the piece, please use the reading "The Problem with YouTube" to support your view. Consequently, please make sure to use at least one quote and one paraphrase with proper in-text citation. Remember, as you are watching the video annotate some notes so you are able to give a brief summary of the video on the discussion board. Please remember, the content of the video must fall into the guidelines of our student conduct code. Please give as much detail in your post as possible, whereas the secondary posting will need your attention to detail to accomplish the second half of our discussion board.

Secondary Posts (100 words each engagement with at least two or more classmates)

When you look for your classmates post on "YouTube" as you present a rebuttal to your peer, based purely on the description, were you able to find their video? If you were able to, could you give more details than your peer original post? Remember, this exercise should be relatively quick; therefore, if you are spending more than 15 minutes looking for the videos, you are either off task, or determined to find a video your peer spoke about in the discussion board. Regardless, time management will be playing a key role in this assignment. Please try to stay on task.

Writing Requirements

- Initial post length: 150–200 words
  - Due by Tuesday at 11:59 p.m.
- Secondary post length: Minimum of 100 words per post (respond to at least two classmates)
  - Due by Sunday at 11:59 p.m.

**Grading is 0% if no submission, or 5% on submission (5 points) – correct criterion will earn 5 points

Assessment Graded 25 Possible Points (5 points each)

Could be either submitted online or in-class pop quiz

Let's Test Your Knowledge – Recall Comprehension

Describe your strategies for reading, and explain the difference in reading one text versus another text. Do you read everything the same? Is everything read at the same pace? For instance, if we are cursory reading, or reading for depth the same amount of time should be given to both process.

Explain "the writing process" in your own words

How would you describe the genre of discussion board assignments?

Describe your own writing process for a discussion board assignment and an essay assignment. In your response, explain how you approach each of these two assignments differently.

Reflect on one of the readings, in doing so, give the author, year and title of the piece; in addition, write a summary of the piece, remember to use in-text citations, as to eliminate plagiarism in your writing sample. As a caveat, write your opinion on the piece, if you "liked or disliked" the reading and you must state "why."

Back to Basics Again and Common Corrections to Writing Strategies

The focus on an academic essay consists of three main sections: Introduction, body, and conclusion, as a "basic writing sample." Whereas many of us have heard of the five-paragraph essay, an **introduction** catches the reader's attention, introduces the topic, and gives the thesis statement. Next, the **body** consists of three paragraphs that develop or explain the argument expressed in the thesis statement through topic sentences, supporting examples/evidence, and good reasons as the **conclusion** closure to the argument by explaining why the argument is important, or by discussing the implications of the argument. Whereas, every essay you write will have the basics included into it for strengthening your format.

Collectively, reiterating of revisions and developing of paragraphs that are needed to be organized around a thesis statement is the support of a topic sentence that states one main idea in each new paragraph, and formulates some sentences that are supported by sufficient, descriptive examples that will illustrate your point. Do not forget the importance of cohesion, continuity, and clarity. Transition will be very important as you develop the discussion posts into an essay, and focus on the connections between paragraphs. In addition, think back and remember the first essay assignment that you were working hard to develop a strong introduction as you capture the reader's attention, creating an effective and well-organized body of text, and finally, an interesting conclusion with a twist of the thesis statement for more dynamics.

The Feedback

Paragraph Development

A New Paragraph should begin a new thought process that contains relevance to the main idea, or topic and the focus of the paragraph. Moreover, all paragraphs should contain a minimum of 3–5 sentences, which are supporting details of the main idea, or topic of the paragraph. This process of breaking down the paragraph is easier for the reader to comprehend.

Paragraph Development

Main paragraph(s) clearly states the dominant impression. The dominant impression contains the topic and the focus of the paragraph. The paragraph effectively develops the dominant impression through a series of well-organized sentences. Typically, it will comprise 5–7 sentences that collectively focus on one topic, and several details to support the topic within the paragraph; all paragraphs contain a topic sentence. Transitional paragraphs will be typically 3–5 sentences, or longer, depending on the details needed to switch smoothly from one topic to another topic.

New paragraph should begin a new thought process that contains relevance to the main idea, or topic and the focus of the paragraph; all paragraphs contain a topic sentence. Moreover, all paragraphs should contain a minimum of 5–7 sentences, and no less than three sentences, which are supporting details of the main idea, or topic of the paragraph. Furthermore, utilizing a transitional word or phrase to join paragraph(s) that contains over 7–10 sentences should be considered for revision, making the process to smaller paragraphs, instead of one large paragraph. This process of breaking down the paragraph is easier for the reader to comprehend the main topic, idea, or claim the writer has created through their intentionality.

Eliminate First Person

Write in third person. Third person allows anyone to become the writer; therefore anyone could tell the story. Therefore, eliminate words such as, "I, me, my, mine, we, ours." A good writer does not identify themselves...the mystery keeps the intrigue of the reader.

Third Person versus First Person

Although writers will enjoy talking about themselves in several different genres, the formal style of writing, or academic writing, should always be completed in third person. Thus, reflecting several points-of-view, eliminating bias, which in turn allow the writer to become an observer, and the reader to adapt, interpret, or formulate the story being told to their own personal viewpoints. In addition, the reader has the understanding of the "I," because you have written the work. Moreover, "I did it" will always be one-sided. Remember, you are more effective as a writer and in creating a writing sample, if "I" does not appear.

Format of Organization: A New Look at the Five-Paragraph Essay

The title page is the first page and includes the class name and number, title of paper, author, and date. Depending on the writing format, a title page may not have a page number and will not be counted in the total pages required.

The introduction (opening paragraph) outlines the purpose or topic of the paper or essay, and the introduction should be considered a brief, concise paragraph of two that summarizes the content of the paper.

The body (the next three supporting paragraphs) is the main section of the paper or essay and includes information based on paragraphs. Remember paragraphs should have one main idea that is in direct support of the thesis statement. Within each body paragraph, there will be a topic sentence (main idea of the paragraph), supporting idea or ideas and an abundance of transition for cohesion.

The conclusion or summary (final paragraph) is the portion of the paper or essay that you will offer a concluding or summarizing comment, or comments. This portion of the paper is a review and tells the reader the outcome of the intent of the writer and the paper means to your perspective of the material read and interpreted on the "readers" behalf.

Discussion 2

Scavenger Hunt

With a small group, please complete the "Library Scavenger Hunt." This task was developed to promote cooperation and collaboration among our classmates or peers. Were you able to meet on campus at an agreed time to accomplish the task?

Remember, this was set-up to be a group activity. Please remember to limit the group. As a reminder, it should be limited to about four people. Was it easy to establish a group leader? Was the activity thwarted from the start of the project? In other words, was the group successful or did someone prevent the group process from happening?

Initial Post (150–200 words)

Please remember to upload your worksheet as part of the discussion. For this activity, **EVERYONE** must submit the initial post, as the group completed the hunt. Please **report the time**, and **members** of your group for the purpose of the activity. In addition, if you had a member that was either assigned into your group or chosen to become a part of your group, but neglected to show for the assignment, or did not "pull their weight," please email me privately.

Each member must upload the work. Moreover, each student must be responsible for their learning. Please do not "cover" up for your peer, as in-class activities will determine if the classmate went on the "scavenger hunt" or not, so the group will take zero versus the individual. **For example**, Bob Smith did not attend class; therefore, he could not be part of the group activity. Nevertheless, at the same time, if an individual was unable to complete the assignment, they should email me privately as well. Please remember to list specific moments, and please make clear and thorough details as you complete the requirement.

Secondary Posts (100 words each with at least two or more classmates)

Please review information listed from within your group, and add details, or another perspective to the event. As the posts are completed, each group should produce a well-rounded perspective of the day.

Writing Requirements

- Initial post length: 150–200 words
  - Due by Tuesday at 11:59 p.m.
- Secondary post length: Minimum of 100 words per post (respond to at least two classmates)
  - Due by Sunday at 11:59 p.m.

**Grading is 0% if no submission, or is 25% on submission (25 points) – correct criterion will earn 25 points

Library Scavenger Hunt

Follow these instructions to complete your onsite visit of the library: Copy or Print the Library Scavenger Hunt

Complete the questions – which will mean that you will have to expand this document to fill in the information. Although fun is "relative," try to remember to have fun today…remember this will be a great resource for your academic career and definitely, as you write. Please post your answers online as part of the discussion board. Lastly, please remember to save the document as "Save as" Library Scavenger Hunt with your name, and the name of your group members – each person must upload to receive credit for the activity.

1. Why use this library at all? What does it have to offer you the student? What do you need to reserve books? **What are the library hours and days of the weeks?** Do they have extended hours during school or modify hours in the summer?

2. **Stop at the Reference Desk.** Look for the library handouts, and ask if there are any of your textbooks on reserve? Ask a reference librarian for assistance. Does the library have any handouts for looking up to reference material? Campus activities? Community activities? Where is the desk located? Was it easy to find? Were there several people in the desk area? What was around the desk?

3. **Locate the Library Lost and Found.** Are there several service desks available to answer questions about research, technology, and for checking out books and paying fines. At which one of these service desks will you find the library Lost and Found? If there is no "lost and found," who gets the items left behind? Place the name here_____

4. **Does the library have a "Technology Help Desk?" If not, where do you get help for Technology issues on campus or from your home if linking to the website?** Find the answer to the questions by talking to the staff:

    a. **Does the library have a FAX machine for student use?** _____
    b. **Does the library have scanners available for student use?** If so, where?_____
    c. **Does the library have copy machines?** Cost of copies?_____
    d. **Where does the library have a color printer?** _____
    e. **Where is the stapler located?**_____
    f. **Are there small rooms for students to meet? Study rooms? Conference rooms?**

5. **Locate the computers, access the OhioLink, and list the different URL/topics you have found… use the first letter to help locate any topics … use the acronym to help find ideas; for example, "The Louvre" (LEARN)…How did you access the OhioLink? Why do you need OhioLink?**

    Give the steps you used to complete the process

    1.

    2.

    3.

    4.

Now as the examples were given in class, please find words that can be searched in the Ohio-link and record the answers. Remember to give the word, the number of searches found for the source, and COPY THE URL (make sure to include all of the important information- this is annotating, and researching)

Example: L – The Louvre (86,268) http://eds.a.ebscohost.com/eds/results?sid=aa65ed9a-5c54 -4169-90b5-3f6b77238dce%40sessionmgr4009&vid=0&hid=4102&bquery=Louvre&bdata=Jn R5cGU9MSZzaXRlPWVkcy1saXZlJnNjb3BlPXNpdGU%3d

L_____

E_____

A_____

R_____

N_____

6. **You already know that for help with writing projects, you can go to the Writing Center. What does the Writing Center not do? Where is the Writing Center located on campus? Is it in the library?** Are there tutors or assistants close by in the library that may give assistance to topics or research?

7. **Take a walk through the building until you exit out the other side...list three things you discovered**

    1. _____

    2. _____

    3. _____

    4. _____

Congratulations on completing your onsite visit to your university Library!

Chapter 6

Community Project/Community Service

Why Complete a Community Service Project?

Consequently, a part of your requirement for completing this course will be for you to become part of a larger cause than just "yourself." As the notion is important, as individuals, we are able to help, guide, and promote civic duties for a greater good.

In addition, you will be asked to research, explore, and fulfill these obligations over the course of our semester, it is good to "see" a general breakdown of the different areas that community service encompasses. Idealistically, you could possibly become our next community leader. Most universities have a program designed to give students an opportunity to experience the "satisfaction" of giving to someone else; they are ensuring that you will be given the opportunity to experience a "civic duty."

Civic Objectives

Please remember, as the assignments are segmented throughout several weeks of the semester; please make sure not to miss the opportunity. Here is an overview of basic civic duties of service.

Purposeful Civic Learning and Community Service have become synonymous with the understanding that the bigger pictures in most things in life are rarely seen if you stare at the object. The same holds true with community service. Here are several of the learning objectives that you may experience throughout the different stages of the project; the development, your involvement, or the reflection needed to culminate the situation. The preparation and participation are part of the students learning process, and there is a value in becoming directly and intentionally involved in a diverse democratic society.

These simple objectives are powerful tools individually, but collectively make for a dynamic intersession of becoming a lifelong learner.

First, you will obtain some "civic skills." The ability to learn, develop competency, and identify community assets. You will learn and develop advocacy skills, as well as different leadership roles. You may even learn where your career fits in the betterment of society.

Second, you will become familiar with "civic knowledge." After conducting research, you should have learned some of the causes to create a social problem and the need for community action. You may possibly learn the effect the change has on communities, and the affect the people have in understanding citizenship. Finally, you should learn the difference between individualism and institutionalism.

Lastly, the use of "civic values" which are the direct implications from underrepresented populations, areas, or community groups. Moreover, you should learn that communities depend on active "citizenry," and the hours saved in a group effort. Finally, and most importantly, understanding the role of the individual, and the leadership process associated with the role versus "certain people just have better characteristics," because most people are responsible for the well-being of others.

Discussion 1

Beginning of a Community Project

Why begin community service? What has my community ever done for me? Here is some things to consider for learning the true value of your community. Once we complete the activity, over the next few classes some of you will learn – Evidence of another students' <u>knowledge of and use of</u> key campus and community resources aligned with desired academic success and personal development and the purpose of a community activity. These strategies will lead to achieve desired academic success and personal development through the utilization of campus and community resources to further academic growth.

Sometimes we need the ***Learning Outcomes Presented in Community Service:***

- Identify key campus resource, which supports academic plan and/or personal development.
- Relate key campus resource to academic plan and/or personal development.
- Demonstrate involvement with identified resource.
- Analyze experience with identified resource against academic plan and/or personal development
- Propose future experience(s) with identified resource

Initial Post (150 words)

The Written Reflection

During this semester, the three most challenging issues I face are_____. In facing these challenges, identify the resources (an individual, campus, or community) and describe how they will assist you. Provide evidence of your use of the campus or community resource (business card, voucher, email from individual, etc.). In addition, please describe your overall experience and remember to reflect in a positive mannerism; whereas, negativity does not merit well, as this was your perception, and there are at least two sides to a story.

Collectively, reflect on the different services available to you and your peers or classmates, and give an example of the strategies you have finished, completed, or "done" to place the resource into your daily, weekly, or monthly schedule. How does this resource help with key Time Management issues that we may face as a college student? Do you feel that this particular resource has made a difference to you as a student? If possible, give the contact information to your resource…your peer may thank you.

Secondary Posts (100 words each post for at least two or more classmates)

As a secondary post, did your peer list a service on/off campus that would help with your overall success, while attending a university. If you have heard of the service, but know of a "better" resource, please include that in your secondary post. Remember to identify your peer, restate a portion of their initial post, and provide support to back up your interpretation.

Writing Requirements

- Initial post length: 150–200 words
  - o Due by Friday at 11:59 p.m.
- Secondary post length: Minimum of 100 words per post (respond to at least two classmates)
  - o Due by Sunday at 11:59 p.m.

**Grading is 0% if no submission, or is 10% on submission – correct criterion will earn 10 points

Assignment: Community Research

For this class or possibly prior and on your own, you have embarked on a Community Service Project. This assignment will entail the use of research, eliminating information, and finding the true relevance to the community, in addition to the services required to keep good civic citizenry.

Listed is the format you should use as you will be conducting research on a given "community service." Please submit the research you have found to support your activity as you served the community. Please reference the format provided to you as an example of types of information that you would provide to the reader. Remember, as a writer you will need to establish details and background information for the reader, so a well-rounded view could be interpreted, as they were part of the event.

Your Community Service Project goes here and the following format will be submitted for grading

(The example provided is The Toledo Animal Shelter – your title and organization will be different)

The Outline

Overview – (Example) Typical Days at the Shelter

Monday

Tuesday

Wednesday

Thursday

Friday

Saturday

Sunday

Essential Job Functions – Type of Programs/Degrees

- For example – Director – Bachelor of Science: Field of Humanitarian Studies Degree required**
- "Requirement" to "work" at the Shelter
-
-
-
-
-

Nonessential Job Functions – List the Jobs within the Organization

-
-
-
-

Requirements – of being a Community Project

- Animals that Qualify to become Part of the Shelter, not all animals are taken into the shelter.
-
-
-
-
-
-

Other Skills/Abilities

-

Record the Research

Research website	What did you know?	What do you want to learn?	What have you learned?

Find at least two or more resources for your particular "Community Service." Please be sure to give enough detail on the information found to give a well-rounded perspective.

For example – The journey of **one animal** and "get" their story…Tucker was a family pet that was given to the rescue the day their owner transferred to another state (TAHS, 2017).

Written Assessment

The **Outline** must be submitted, as well as the written information found in the research of a community program. Furthermore, the information presented in your **writing sample** must contain the community event, the name of the organization, and a summary of the research. Proper grammar/sentence structure should be found throughout the written work. In addition, all references included within the work should be reflected with proper in-text citation, as well as the reference page. Remember, failure to cite your work properly could result in plagiarism.

Assessment and Grading – Upload the Assignment

Writing Requirements (APA format)

- 1–2 pages (approx. 300 words per page – 5–7 paragraphs per page)
- 1-inch margins
- Double-spaced
- 12-point Times New Roman font
- Cover page
- Reference page
- Due date: By 11:59 p.m. on Sunday

**Grading is 0% if no submission, or is 25% on submission – correct criterion will earn 25 points

Civic Duty – Discussion 2

Community Service and Civic Objectives

Whereas, part of your requirement for completing this course, we require you to become part of a larger cause than just "yourself." The notion is important as we individuals are able to help, guide, and promote civic duties for a greater good. As you will research, explore, and fulfill these obligations over the semester, it is good to "see" a general breakdown of the different areas that community service encompasses. So you could possibly become our next community leader.

Most universities have a program designed to give students an opportunity to experience the "satisfaction" of giving to someone else, we are ensuring that you will be given the opportunity. Please remember, as the assignments are segmented throughout several weeks of the semester; please make sure not to miss the opportunity.

Purposeful Civic Learning and Community Service

Learning that directly and intentionally prepares students for active civic participation in a diverse democratic society.

Grading

Participation only – 20 points or 0 point (up to 20%)

Initial Post (150–200 words)

Please remember as part of the discussion for this activity, you must have been present. **EVERYONE** must submit the initial post, as the group completed the community service together. This is a reflection of the event, participation, and collaboration of your community service.

Each member must upload the work. In addition, each student must be responsible for their learning, please do not "cover" up for your peer, as in-class activities will determine if the classmate was able to list specific moments, give details. Please make sure that these details are clear and thorough as you complete the post. Remember, each of you will have a different perspective to the activity that unfolds.

Secondary posts (100 words each with at least two or more classmates)

Please review information listed from within your group, and add details, or another perspective to the event. As the posts are completed, each group should produce a well-rounded perspective of the day.

Writing Requirements

- Initial post length: 150–200 words
  - Due by Tuesday at 11:59 p.m.
- Secondary post length: Minimum of 100 words per post (respond to at least two classmates)
  - Due by Sunday at 11:59 p.m.

**Grading is 0% if no submission, or is 20% on submission – correct criterion will earn 20 points

Assignment – Academic Essay

Drafting Arguments

Often, as you think about writing, we focus on the drafting phrase. Drafting is the process of cobbling your ideas together in sentences and paragraphs. The aim of the drafting phase is to develop something that looks like a full text, though that text is usually not ready for submission when it is first completed. Drafting is usually not a one-time shot in which a student sits down for an hour or two and busts out a full-fledged essay of 6–8 pages! Instead, like most everything else related to writing, it is a process of its own. Successful students work in lots of revision as they draft – students may write a sentence or paragraph, then immediately revise it, or write a section of the essay, then come back later to make changes in the organization, development, etc. Drafting is thus a rather intense phase that requires lots of sustained attention and larger blocks of time.

Therefore, thinking about the situations in which you write will be worth the time you invest. Consider, for example, these questions: Think about the last essay that you wrote. Where did you write it? At home? In the library? At a coffee shop? At work? Where were you sitting, and what was going on around you? Were your kids fighting over some toy in the next room? Was the TV on? Were you listening to music? What time of day was it? Early in the morning, in the afternoon, or late at night after work was finished? How did you feel? Were you tired from work or taking care of the kids? Did you just finish preparing dinner and cleaning up? Were you tired from working the night before, or were you fresh from a good night's rest?

Whatever your circumstances are, it is worthwhile to be aware of your usual practices and to make any changes in the conditions in which you work. Ideally, you should try to write when your body and mind are fresh – for most people, this happens early in the morning. Try to set aside chunks of time to work on your essay. Set clear goals for yourself as a writer for each writing session. Do your best to build in enough time to outline, organize, reread, revise, and edit your writing before the due date!

Academic Essay

Remember, an academic essay consists of three main sections: Introduction, body, and conclusion. Many of us have heard of the five-paragraph essay: an **introduction** catches the reader's attention, introduces the topic, and gives the thesis statement. The **body** consists of three paragraphs that develop or explain the argument expressed in the thesis statement through topic sentences, supporting examples/evidence, and good reasons, and the **conclusion** closure to the argument by explaining why the argument is important, or by discussing the implications of the argument.

The draft of this assignment will draw on information learned up to this point to be able to develop paragraphs that are organized around a topic sentence that states one main idea, and are supported by sufficient, descriptive examples that illustrate your point. As you had developed the discussion posts into an essay, focus on the connections between paragraphs. In addition, for this first essay assignment, work to develop a strong introduction, an effective and well-organized body, and an interesting conclusion.

The Assignment

Write an essay that discusses the concept you defined in an Essay. For example, Christian (2011) "The Problem with You Tube," now you will argue the facts you found in your research, remember you need two additional sources. In order to expand your thoughts into a longer essay, you might want to consider one of the following strategies:

- Discuss why this information is important and should be used in 21st century American society.
- Explain and evaluate the implications of the information that you have researched in the Essay.
- Explore the causes and/or effects of the information that you have researched in the Essay for our society.

Rhetorical Situation – Different Way of Writing it...

The rhetorical situation refers to the relationship between various forces that affect any given text written to be read. Whereas, understanding the rhetorical situation of the text you are writing can help you make better choices related to the kinds of language, examples, and arguments that you use in your essay. Consider, for example, the kinds of language you would use on Facebook compared to the kinds of language you would use on a résumé. Think about how you would argue that you deserve a raise to your boss compared to how you would argue that you deserve a raise to a close friend on the other hand. Paying attention to the rhetorical situation can help us understand the complex relationships between the reader, writer, text, and message.

The components of a rhetorical situation include the **text** (content, words, images, form, media), the **reader** (who brings knowledge, experience, memories, predictions, feelings, and desires to the act of reading), the **writer** (who also brings knowledge, experience, memories, feelings, intentions, purposes, and desires to the act of writing), and a **context** (which includes textual, immediate, and historical and social factors). Rhetoric is the art of understanding textual events by considering its rhetorical situation.

For example, consider this lecture. It is a text and has its own rhetorical situation.

First, let us look at the **text**: a series of sentences, paragraphs, and terms (some of which are highlighted in bold font). The content of this lecture is related to the main concepts of "analysis" and "rhetorical situation." Remember, the argument will be clearly stated without ever using the words, "I agree, or I disagree."

The **writer** is "I" or simply stated me. I am a scholar of literacy, rhetoric, and composition. I have degrees in English literature, literacy, rhetoric, and composition. I bring to the moment of writing this lecture a wealth of knowledge in these areas that I have collected as a student, teacher, and researcher. I also bring a great deal of experience as a writer. My purpose in writing this lecture is to educate others about the concept of a "rhetorical situation," and I desire to do that in a personal, informative, and professional manner.

You are the **reader**, but you are also many. Each of you brings a different set of experiences, knowledge, memories, etc. to the moment of reading this lecture. However, all of you are money-paying students interested in getting something out of reading this lecture: a grade, a degree, a job.

Surrounding both of us (readers and writer) are various **contexts** – I am writing this in the summer of 2011. You are reading it sometime after that point. My immediate context includes a deadline to complete this work. Your immediate context includes understanding these concepts so that you can complete other assignments. However, we also have other factors affecting us – I am hungry and want to stop working on this so that I can go have lunch. I will not get home until late tonight and am anxious to clean my house, but I do not feel like I have time. My son has to go to the eye doctor, and I am worried about the cost of getting new glasses. What are the immediate contexts affecting you?

Making Arguments

There are three strategies for appealing to your audience: **ethos,** or appeal to **credibility, pathos,** or appeal to **emotions,** and **logos,** or appeal to **reason.** The **rhetorical** appeals are **types of arguments** that we make. For instance, we might say in everyday situations phrases like: "Believe me when I say that place is no good!" (Ethos); "If you buy this product for me, I will be happy" (Pathos); and "Buy two because you will save 30%" (Logos). Nevertheless, how do we develop these arguments into practice?

Assessment and Grading

Writing Requirements (APA format)

- 2–3 pages
- 1-inch margins
- Double-spaced
- 12-point Times New Roman font
- Title page
- Reference page (should include one book/Sources – 2 to 3 Ohiolink)
- Due date: Sunday by 11:59 p.m.

**Grading is 0% if no submission, or is 65% on submission – correct criterion will earn 65 points

Chapter 7

Patterns of Organization

Lecturette Notes

Understanding the Process of Organization

Just as the "reader" will use "patterns of organization" to collect information to develop comprehension of a text, that information will be remembered, recalled, recited, or reviewed in the future. The same holds true as many authors or "writers" use "patterns of organization" to "get their point across" to the reader, "reader–writer" connection develops…recognizing the main idea or claim and the purpose will help you identify the details supporting the main idea, and determine the specific pattern of the writing sample.

Importantly, looking for details, referred to as support or evidence throughout writing samples, tends to focus on four main points, which could be presented as an example, statistic, testimony (eye-witness account), and reasons. Types of examples are through personal experience, public experience (societal view), hypothetical scenario, and facts. Statistical analyses should always be reviewed with caution, as the "statistician" has the ability to create data based on population, variation, and "sought outcome." Therefore, if the data set changes the validity of the results may become skewed or irrelevant as the information becomes erroneous with new results. Testimony presents the "opinion" or emotional state of being from another, statements of experts, or just their personal point-of-view. Finally, reasons are usually associated with logic, are sensible explanations viewed through deduction (general/global view to specific idea), or induction (specific idea to general/global view), and will typically answer the question of "why."

Nevertheless, as we prepare "patterns" and present the information to another, there should be a logical order to our thinking, strategies, and overall conveying of information for the audience, whether as the reader or the receptor (listener). As we present an experience, try to look at it as the "big picture," to have greatest impact as the writer. As the importance from the concepts found in the chapters, remember the overview of essential details, the main idea from each unit, and any skills that will be necessary, such as the visual aids. Finally, ask any questions relevant to creating a deeper level of thinking.

Consequently, the same principle affects us as readers and writers. Remember, if things are laid out and sorted in order, we have the ability to work with them more easily. Keep in mind, it is easier to "tell a story" from the beginning to the end, versus just giving pieces of details in a sporadic order, hence the story needs order to "unfold" properly for it to be understood. This will help your reader make a connection, discover relationships between the main idea and details, most of all create cohesion of your thoughts.

Patterns of Organization as The Reader…The Writer…The Interpreter

1.   Cause and Effect (also as the writer)

Cause and effect is utilized to demonstrate a causal relationship (positive or negative) between an event and its impact, or as something has happened and the outcome. Sometimes one cause (reason) can have only one effect (consequence); however, please remember there are multiple effects for multiple causes, and vice versa, which will show causal relations between events and their impact. Therefore, the outcome may reflect with a positive or negative result.

2.   Chronological Order (also as the writer)

Chronological order or time order is information arranged in the order in which the event occurred, and the information presented over time or steps that needs to be taken in sequence. The best way to differentiate between chronological order and process is "think of a time line." For example, you are born in 1992; consequently, in 1993 you should be walking around the house.

3.   Classification/Analyze (also as the writer)

Classification or analysis is a simple pattern to place ideas into categories according to their characteristics (grouping), or dividing a "single entity" (whole) into parts. Whereas, "science class" may have had the students separate leaves or rocks and place them into similar groups; hence, students classified the specimens based on their similarities, and were more likely to remember these because of multiple cognitive functions required for critical thought.

4.   Comparison and Contrast (also as the writer)

Comparison and contrast are techniques used to point out similarities (comparison) and differences (contrast), or possibly use both to show there are "things that are alike, and dislike in relation to each other." Recognizing the ability for topics to alternate, or go back and forth, or stating all traits before moving to the next idea, or a difference among topics. For example, customer, consumer, patient, and client collectively the words are all similar in nature as each represents people and service; nevertheless, each has a very different meaning based on ideology, as a customer shops for service, a consumer buys or uses a service, a patient receives a service, a client pays for a service.

5.   Definition (also as the writer)

Definition is provided as a means to show example by defining the term, idea, concept, or topic, whereas introduction of more than one term is a possibility. Primarily used in "technical writing," it is often found in textbooks to reinforce "unfamiliar vocabulary" to the reader, as the "context clues" may need stronger reinforcement for coherency. Whereas the writing sample becomes similar to "information commonly found in a dictionary," as specific examples that distinguish "characteristics" apart from all others, think of the entry as "Webster" would record it.

6.   Illustration/Example (also as the writer)

Illustration or example is given in writing to create a more concrete understanding of a "complex phe-nomenon," abstract concept or difficult term. Therefore, "drawing a picture" creates the assimilation for the reader to retain information necessary for comprehension, especially in identifying the key concepts or main idea. Consequently, providing the reader with very descriptive words to provide a location or setting to establish cohesiveness of a "tangible" object produced within an "intangible world," you could appeal to the "senses," such as using sight, smell, sound, taste, or touch. For example, as Bonnie walked into the room, say smoke, she immediately looked for flames on the floor, ceiling, and walls; as there was lack of evidence of fire, she began to crawl on hands, and knees toward the door, and then the odor of burnt marshmallows…Bob and Jim were toasting them over a fire outside.

7.   Listing/Addition

Listing or Addition is the use of words that guide a process, arrange information that lacks a specific order, or creates sporadic ideas on a "sound board." As you try to remember this pattern "think of Santa Claus," where he has made a list "and checked it twice." This process does not replace "chronological order or process"; each of these has a very specific need in writing.

8.   Process/Narrative (also as the writer)

Process arranges information in an order according to the "process" needed to accomplish a task, or as a "process occurs over time." Consequently, the pattern will look similar to "chronological order"; however, instead of overtime; the writer describes steps necessary for building, installing, drafting, creating, and the like to show direction and guidance for the reader. Narrative arranges "a story" with the intension of key concepts, thought interject or details that unfold over time, events support the content, and becomes descriptive so that the "picture" becomes clearer, and the reader has the ability to "envision it."

9.   Spatial Order

Spatial order creates details according to "space," and shows a pattern in regards to a layout, direction, or location; in addition, it guides the reader to visualize a person, place, or thing, and uses descriptive language to produce a "vivid image." Therefore, utilizing the words, up, down, left, right, bottom, top, north, south, inside, and outside will guide the reader to a "specific reference point" in "space."

10. Statement and Clarification

Statement and clarification are used to make "critical thought" manageable for the reader, such as the deductive and inductive reasoning that produces logic to the reader; a general idea is presented and then the writer expounds on it to create an understanding of the idea for the reader, which in turn presents a clear interpretation of the "author's intention."

Deductive reasoning occurs as the "researcher" looks from the more "broader" topic, or informa-tion toward more specific observation; often referred to as the "top-down" approach in theory to reach a conclusion. For example, as I leave for work today at eight o'clock in my car, it takes 45 minutes, and I arrived on time; therefore, I will be on time if I always leave at eight o'clock. However, this statement does leave a margin for error, as if a school bus leaves off children, and the children take 10 minutes to load the bus, then you will be late for work. Consequently, there is a premise for the original "hypothesis" to wrong the possibility of the unknown will always be present.

Inductive reasoning is just the opposite, as idea moves from a specific observation to broader generalizations, and sometimes referred to as "bottom-down" approach. Therefore, I leave at eight o'clock, and arrived on time. Concurrently, every day I would leave my house at eight o'clock, then I will always be on time. This type of reasoning is often found "in science" or more commonly used is "not always logically valid," because the accuracy "assumes" the general or broader idea is correct, whereas it is not always accurate at all.

11. Exemplify (as the writer)

Exemplification is the use of a "general point" to become a "specific point" through an explanation by the use of examples within a writing sample. For example, the idea of washing clothes, or "laundry" should be a simple task, whereas the collections of clothes should be in a specific location; nevertheless, as the items of clothing are placed in an eclectic array throughout the house, the use of a "laundry basket or hamper" must be used to ensure "good use of time" on laundry day. Therefore, clothes should be placed into a hamper, instead of sporadically placed or dropped as to the "last place standing." Lastly, the time spent on "laundry" should be less than an hour a day, therefore making the task simple.

12. Reaction (writing technique)

Reaction is used primarily as the writer creates a statement in which "opinion or personal views are incorporated into the writing sample," and the "writer" has knowledge, or experience directly related to the material. Therefore, as the focus is simple, the "actions" create the need to evaluate a situation with "critical thought," problem-solving, examination of material. In addition, the experience has a direct relation to the subject or topic, and requires the reader to interpret or understand the intention of the "writer," and avoid misinterpretation, which will misrepresent the original intention of the writer.

Discussion – Argument

For this week our topics are quite different from Mullich (2004) "Should You Eat by the Numbers," and Moss (2007) "The Extraordinary Science of Addictive Junk Food." As seen in both pieces, food tends to be the "hot topic." As both authors create an opinion of their topic, please make sure you review your view of either for or against their main idea. Please remember to support your thoughts with proper in-text citations. As you begin to write your discussion, you will review both of these pieces, but remember you must, if your opinion matches theirs, to incorporate into the writing sample the in-text citations that matches your view to support your opinion.

Initial Post

150–200 words based on your perspective of both of the given readings. For the discussion that you will "argue," please make sure that your thesis statement reflects the argument. In addition, you will write your piece with the idea that the reader has limited or no prior knowledge of the topic. Please do not place the words: "I agree, or I disagree." Just make your relevant points. Remember to re-read your work before you post it into the discussion board. This will be similar to your opening paragraph, which will be found in your rough draft, or final draft. Remember the main idea is to "think."

Here are some questions you may want to reflect in the initial post:

1. Where should we draw the line between addictions and genuine need for food?
2. Is there a difference in "junk food" or is this a generic label?
3. Is there a difference in the degree of "how much is consumed – or just inability to control our appetites?"
4. Does the word "addiction" make a connection to food or do you think it is purely "drug usage?"
5. Does Moss's work on the food industry suggest that there should be more responsibility to them, and the consumer is innocent and the "victim?"
6. Mullich (2004) stated that eating by numbers will help eliminate "fat" and the "ideal weight," do you think they are correct.
7. Mullich (2004) discusses the "South Beach Diet," why are "fad diets" so "unhealthy?"
8. Is food just a "social interaction," or necessity?

Secondary Posts (100 words each for at least two or more peers or classmates in the discussion board)

For the secondary post, please critique your peer to see if the main point of their argument is clearly understood in the writing sample. If you agree with your peer, please state why you agree; consequently, if you disagree please state why. As a more challenging counter discussion, please take the other view of your peer, and see if you are able to argue for the other side. Remember to stay positive in all posts, and use proper English in the discussion board with in-text citation to support your theory; more importantly, use some of your peers work to re-state their idea for a stronger debate.

Here are Some Questions You Should Pose to Your Peer

1. Was their argument effective?
2. Did you understand the information provided to you regarding both readings?
3. If you only had their opinion to support the rest of your life in "eating habits," could you do it?

Good Reasons Explain an Argument – Here are Some Standard Rhetorical Arguments

- **Reject counter arguments:** A highly effective strategy is to acknowledge the counter arguments to your position, and give reasons your argument is better. For instance, "While many people say that tuition is high, the value of the education you receive is not easily quantified."
- **Argue by definition:** Can you frame something in terms of another thing? A definition argument uses the pattern "X *is a* Y" to draw connections between two seemingly disparate concepts. For example, "We should ban the death penalty because capital punishment is murder" argues that capital punishment is like murder. This approach is effective because while your audience may not necessarily agree with you that capital punishment should be banned, they will be ready to agree with you that murder is bad for a society, and that anything like murder is probably not good, and should therefore be made illegal.
- **Argue from value:** Say that something is a good or bad something else. An evaluative argument uses the pattern "X is a *good/bad* Y" to express a judgment of value about something. For example, the argument that "Eating out three times a week is a bad way to cut down on your food budget" rejects "eating out" as an expensive practice.
- **Argue by comparing or contrasting:** Help your reader clarify multiple sides by comparing or contrasting the objects of analysis. To express a comparison or contrast, use this pattern: "X is/is not like Y." For example, "Burger King Shakes are unlike McDonalds Shakes because they are creamier."
- **Argue from consequence:** Often, an effective way to persuade your readers is to show that certain *bad things* will happen, or certain *good things* will not happen as a result of something else. For instance, "If we shut down the government, millions of poor children will lose access to the healthcare they depend on, which could result in premature loss."

Assessment and Grading

Writing Requirements – See Rubric

- Initial post length: 150–200 words
  - Due by Tuesday at 11:59 p.m.
- Secondary post length: Minimum of 100 words per post (respond to at least two classmates)
  - Due by Sunday at 11:59 p.m.

**Grading is 0% if no submission, or is 25% on submission– correct criterion will earn 25 points

Interactive/Experiential Lecturettes

Why are the lecturettes so helpful to students? Lecturettes are an excellent way for students to learn and to share knowledge they have gathered in a course, lecture, or general information. Consequently, in turn the student has obtained to make the educational process to have a deeper impact on the overall individual student's success. Inductively, lecturettes are designed to promote an active learner versus a passive learner.

Moreover, the concept itself was designed to help individuals integrate personal learning with a conceptual process and to use material based on theory and research; concurrently, the individual will use the inputs from other members of the class, group, or participants, focus on it, and develop an awareness of theories and research that may have only created "surface learning." In other words, as the individuals research, learn, and recite the knowledge gained, the interaction among peers promotes collaborative learning within a classroom.

Similar to a "think aloud" approach, the facilitator is the student who reveals the principles, models, research, and theories that will evolve around the proposed topics chosen for the week. Remember, you are the one presenting information for your peers to know the important facts and the author's intentionality. So, you must be well versed in the reading, article, or topic presented to the class.

We can have an overview of the different types of lecturettes you may choose from in order to complete the task. In addition, you may have chosen to work with a partner on the assignment. The overall presentation is truly the "accomplishment" as you will have the opportunity to become, learner, student, recitalist, and facilitator for the given readings. Remember, you can choose any two readings; they may be from past readings or those already covered to new topics yet to be explored within our class, which could probably be more interesting to hear, as you will be developing background knowledge for your classmates.

Fruition and integration of personal learning with conceptual material based on theory and research findings are among the most important objectives of "human relations training." Therefore, people integrate with others and the community support is needed to succeed in academics. Everyone cannot read everything, but this does not mean the information is not valid to expand on or share for the betterment of a class.

Lastly, providing individuals with the tools toward production and assimilation creates an approach that becomes an "experiential lecture" or "interactive lecturette". In other words, the lecture "material" is cultivated in the learners. Regardless, keep in mind, you as the facilitator's will have the task to tap that material, to focus it, and to make it come alive conceptually. In addition, lecturettes may also be used to provide short statements of principles, models, research findings, or theories being reviewed within specific disciplines. They "provide stimuli" to which peers and classmates have the chance responds with new levels of awareness.

How to Make a Lecturette

With a little imagination, the facilitator can make almost any conceptual input experiential. The primary advantages for doing so are as follows:

Make Involvement Happen

In general, it is important to design any training activity in such a way as to avoid putting participants in a passive posture because commitment can result only from a sense of ownership through meaningful involvement.

Relevance is Important – Stick to the Facts

It is difficult to anticipate what will be significant to each member of a group.

When participants are engaged in activities correlated with conceptual input, they make the content immediately credible for themselves.

Expanding the Database – Outsource your Material

Using experiential techniques in conjunction with lecturettes capitalizes on the experience pool (both in the "here and now" and "there and then"), which exists within the participant group.

Two-way communication – Facilitator Uses the "Think Aloud"

The facilitator can have effective communication when the content is clear, and two-way exchanges are much more likely to meet this criterion than one-way telling.

Do you know what just happened? Checking understanding – Ask the Audience Questions

Since considerable screening of information occurs as participants listen to a lecturette, experiential exchanges help the facilitator to determine the accuracy of the communication, isolate any misunderstanding of concepts, and correct possible misconceptions.

Maintaining Rapport – Let's Reflect on the Material and Include Real-life Events

Presenting concepts inputs can create a sense of distance between the facilitator and the group. By maintaining an open relationship with the group, the facilitator can challenge the learners in a nonthreatening way to look within themselves for conceptual models, rather relying on the "export" to provide the answers.

Excitement – Say it with Intonation

Participants are more likely to be receptive to input that they experience in a lively manner.

Interactive/Experiential Lecturettes

Lecturettes are an excellent way for us to learn and to share knowledge they have gathered in a course, lecture, or general information; consequently, in turn we have obtained to make the educational process to have a deeper impact on the overall individual's success. Inductively, lecturettes are designed to promote an active learner versus a passive learner. Moreover, the concept itself was designed to help individuals integrate personal learning with a conceptual process to use material based on theory and research; concurrently, the individual will use the inputs from other members of the class, group, or participants, focus on it, and develop an awareness of theories and research that may have only created "surface learning." In other words, as the individuals research, learn, and recite the knowledge gained, the interaction among peers promotes collaborative learning within a classroom. Similar to a "think aloud" approach, the facilitator is the student who reveals the principles, models, research, and theories that will evolve around the proposed topics chosen for the week.

We can have an overview of the different types of lecturettes we may choose from in order to complete the task. In addition, you may have chosen to work with a partner on the assignment. The overall presentation is truly the "accomplishment" as you will have the opportunity to become learner, student, recitalist, and facilitator for the given readings. Remember, you will chose any two readings; they may be from past readings or those already covered to new topics yet to be explored within our class, which could probably be more interesting to hear.

Even so, the integration of personal learning with conceptual material based on theory and research findings is among the most important objectives of "human relations training." Providing us with the tools toward production and assimilation creates an approach that becomes an "experiential lecture" or "interactive lecturette". In other words, the lecture "material" is cultivated in the learners. Regardless, keep in mind, you as the facilitator will have the task to tap that material, to focus it, and to make it come alive conceptually. In addition, lecturettes may also be used to provide short statements of principles, models, research findings, or theories being reviewed within specific disciplines. They "provide stimuli" to which peers and classmates have the chance to respond with new levels of awareness.

How to Make a lecturette

With a little imagination, the facilitator can make almost any conceptual input experiential. The primary advantages for doing so are as follows:

Involvement

In general, it is important to design any training activity in such a way as to avoid putting participants in a passive posture because commitment can result only from a sense of ownership through meaningful involvement.

Relevance

It is difficult to anticipate what will be significant to each member of a group.

When participants are engaged in activities correlated with conceptual input, they make the content immediately credible for themselves.

Expanding the Database

Using experiential techniques in conjunction with lecturettes capitalizes on the experience pool (both in the "here and now" and "there and then"), which exists within the participant group.

Two-way Communication

The facilitator can have effective communication when the content is clear, and two-way exchanges are much more likely to meet this criterion than one-way telling.

Checking Understanding

Since considerable screening of information occurs as participants listen to a lecturette, experiential exchanges help the facilitator to determine the accuracy of the communication, isolate any misunderstanding of concepts, and correct possible misconceptions.

Maintaining Rapport

Presenting concepts inputs can create a sense of distance between the facilitator and the group. By maintaining an open relationship with the group, the facilitator can challenge the learners in a nonthreatening way to look within themselves for conceptual models, rather relying on the "export" to provide the answers.

Excitement

Participants are more likely to be receptive to input that they experience in a lively manner.

Assignment

For our lecturette, please pick two stories from either books presented as part of the course material, and base it on the principles of using patterns of organization. For example, the use of Compare and Contrast, Problem-Solving, Argument, Persuasion, Cause and Effect, Chronological, Listing-Enumeration, or another strategy used for reading patterns or writing patterns. Please refer the "organizational charts" located in the "organizational charts folder."

Presentations will begin promptly...typically in the next class (date will be provided in class)

The lecturette will be presented in class using the same rubric within our class. Please make sure you come prepared to the classroom, as the assignment of order will be determined on the day of presentation. As a caveat, please make sure to email yourself any power points, and material being used to enhance the presentation, as not all flash drives may be compatible with every computer system on campus.

Assessment and Grading

Writing Requirements (APA format)

- 2–3 pages (approximately 300 words per page)
- 1-inch margins
- Double-spaced
- 12-point Times New Roman font
- Title page
- Reference page (should include two book sources for readings)
- Due date: Sunday by 11:59 p.m.

Assignment – Let's Share

Objective: Student's ability to comprehend, share knowledge, and develop background knowledge for their peers. In addition, the ability to record, summarize readings, and produce an effective writing sample to represent the author's intentionality.

Review the Basics of the Lecturette

Lecturettes are an excellent way for us to learn and to share knowledge they have gathered in a course, lecture, or general information; consequently, in turn we have obtained to make the educational process to have a deeper impact on the overall individual's success. Inductively, lecturettes are designed to promote an active learner versus a passive learner. Moreover, the concept itself was designed to help individuals integrate personal learning with a conceptual process to use material based on theory and research; concurrently, the individual will use the inputs from other members of the class, group, or participants, focus on it, and develop an awareness of theories, and research that may have only created "surface learning." In other words, as the individual's research, learn, and recite the knowledge gained, the interaction among peers promotes collaborative learning within a classroom. Similar to a "think aloud" approach, the facilitator is the student who reveals the principles, models, research, and theories that will evolve around the proposed topics chosen for the week.

We can have an overview of the different types of lecturettes we may choose from in order to complete the task. In addition, you may have chosen to work with a partner on the assignment. The overall presentation is truly the "accomplishment" as you will have the opportunity to become learner, student, recitalist, and facilitator for the given readings. Remember, you will choose any two readings; they may be from past readings or those already covered to new topics yet to be explored within our class, which could probably be more interesting to hear.

Even so, the integration of personal learning with conceptual material based on theory and research findings is among the most important objectives of "human relations training." Providing us with the tools toward production and assimilation creates an approach that becomes an "experiential lecture" or "interactive lecturette." In other words, the lecture "material" is cultivated in the learners. Regardless, keep in mind, you as the facilitator will have the task to tap that material, to focus it, and to make it come alive conceptually. In addition, lecturettes may also be used to provide short statements of principles, models, research findings, or theories being reviewed within specific disciplines. They "provide stimuli" to which peers and classmates have the chance responds with new levels of awareness.

Assignment (Written and Material Presented in Class)

For our lecturette there are two parts for completing the assignment. Please pick two stories from either books presented as part of the course material, and base it on the principles of using patterns of organization. For example, the use of Compare and Contrast, Problem-Solving, Argument, Persuasion, Cause and Effect, Chronological, Listing-Enumeration, or another strategy used for reading patterns or writing patterns. Please refer the "organizational charts" and remember that a written submission of the lecturettes must be submitted to receive credit.

Presentations will begin promptly …typically in the next class (date will be provided in class)

The lecturette will be presented in class using the same rubric within our class. Please make sure you come prepared to the classroom, as the assignment of order will be determined on the day of presentation. As a caveat, please make sure to email yourself any power points, and material being used to enhance the presentation, as not all flash drives may be compatible with every computer system on campus.

Writing Assessment and Grading (Possible 100 total points)

Writing Requirements (APA format)

- 2–3 pages (approximately 300 words per page)
- 1-inch margins
- Double-spaced
- 12-point Times New Roman font
- Title page
- Reference page (should include two book sources for readings)
- Due date: Sunday by 11:59 p.m.

**Grading is 0% if no submission, else 50% on submission (50 points) – correct criterion will earn 50 points

Presentation Grading - **Grading is 0% no submission or is 50% submission (50 points) – correct criterion will earn 50 points

Presentation rubric - will be discussed in class.

Chapter 8

Writing Process

The Process of Writing

Let us we review the writing process, please think of all the terms you may already be familiar with in English. Whereas, each process of writing has different steps that will not always reflect a linear process, as the editing, revising, and polishing may interchange, and change again, before the finished product is at hand. Here are a list of terms used in the writing process. Remember, we began this process in the very first chapter, and have been practicing the process ever since.

Writing Process Terms

Brainstorm

Outline

Prewrites

Drafts/Revision

Proof Read

Rewrite

Fluency (transitional words or phrases)

Polish

Product

Writing Process Steps and Important Concepts that Connect with Reading Anything

What is writing?

In 21st century American society, we write all the time – whether in a journal, on a cell phone, or on Facebook, we use writing to connect with others and ourselves; however, the context read could be very misleading.

Ask Yourself these Simple Questions:

1. How would you define writing? What does writing mean other than forming letters and words?
2. Why are you required to take reading and writing classes in a college or university?

First, let us reflect that **writing** is very similar to spoken language in many ways, but we do not write and speak the same.

- Audience: The person or people (most frequently) speak/write to other people
- Purpose: Speech/writing/oral communication is used to do all sorts of things, such as give a command, ask a question, provide direction, deliver information, and classify items.
- Context is the way we say/write and it is situated into broader (general) or more focused (narrow) conversations and circumstances that provide facts, ideas, concepts, or topics to be heard or viewed by another person.

Developing a Deeper Meaning to Rhetoric and Oratory Applications

Be Mindful

Many people often talk without giving much "thought" to "what" we say; unless we are giving a speech, we rarely "plan" or "organize" our processes. Hence, please think before speaking. Usually, writing demands critical thinking of "what" we want to say and "how" to organize it very carefully for our readers.

Use Proper Body

Most people rely heavily on body language and facial expressions to convey our ideas while speaking. Although we cannot read or see body language while reading another's text, writing is an embodied process. Often, writers experience cycles of frustration and confidence throughout the entire writing process (from developing ideas to submitting the final product) as they write longer texts, such as essays. Nevertheless, the practice of writing does create more opportunities for creativity and reflection of other perspectives.

Take a Look Around the World

Whereas most people talk to others, their language is always "out there, in the world," which means that there are broader contexts that affect the way we speak (how) and responses we can say (what) as a rebuttal in conversation. For example, at work, the demands of a particular profession or the presence of a boss may change the way an exchange of words is held about something. Consequently, our audience is not always in front of us if we write, their expectations still have an impact on our final products. For instance, an essay must be written for a class, the chosen language going print is very different, if the topic would be written on Facebook. Positively, at least it should! Consider the difference: one is formal, the other is informal.

Giving Enough Time and/or Taking Too Much Space

Usually, people talk in "real time" in a synchronous fashion (through face-to-face conversations, or conversations over the phone and/or live internet) versus some online course, which is asynchronous. However, these conversations happen (more or less) at the same time – someone may say something. For example, I say something, and then we may say something at the same time. Besides, if we speak face-to-face, we share a common space.

Albeit, the written word constructed over time is split or fractured, meaning that I may write (say) something a month before you read (hear) it. Also, we very rarely share reading/writing spaces; most people typically move from a writing "spot" to the reading "spot." Therefore, to write in multiple areas (office, coffee shop, work), and to read in several places (kitchen, car, restaurant), do not reflect the same "spot."

Understanding Writing – Once you understand "how" writing is affected by these factors, personally can make adjustments in your writing samples. To learn writing, you have to recognize "how" writing occurs across all of these categories:

Prewriting Strategies

Use prewriting strategies to discover ideas, to find the argument, and to come up with details for an essay, paper, research topic or report.

- Audience/Context/Purpose
- Mind/Body/World
- Space/Time
- Brainstorming
- Idea mapping
- Freewriting
- Thinking

Drafting

The drafting process is the stage to write a draft. However, during this phase, consider continuing to use prewriting strategies and most certainly, revision strategies as you work to put an essay together. The first draft should not "look like" the last draft (final product).

- Outlining
- Reading
- Writing

Revising

Revision is a crucial part of the writing process because at this stage we reflect and pause for a moment to think about clarity – do your ideas make sense to other people? Unless others can read and understand, the argument or claim being stated will not be successful. This stage often involves a lot of reading and re-drafting. Caution! Try to make all revisions after a short break from the writing process; otherwise, the words intended to be read may not be on the page; oddly, the mind silently reads intent and not always the print.

- Re-reading
- Re-organizing content
- Re-writing for clarity

Proofreading or Editing

In this final stage of the writing process, the attention from big-picture revision concerns like clarity, and the organization must begin on the practical details; focus on syntax, grammar, and structure. Have I placed commas in the right places? Did I spell everything correctly? Lastly, do it one more time, and read the writing sample backward. This will catch "correct spelling" errors (homonym – write/right; a homophone – to, two, too, or a homograph – so, and yet there are many others).

- Re-reading for grammar, mechanics, punctuation, and spelling
- Re-writing for style

Discussion

For this week as we try to get back in the "swing of things," this discussion will be a reflective piece to help "stir" that prior knowledge you had as you began this course, and recall background knowledge learned as a participant in our college reading class. Please be sure to review the "Lectures" as they contain information as a reinforcement of our daily in-class engagements.

Initial Post (150–200 words)

To begin our week, please take time to reflect on past discussions, lectures, peer critiques, and assignments. Please take the time to think about your different expectations you may have had prior to the start of the course. As you reflect, think about the readings, and your role as the writer. Please give no less than a paragraph of items you enjoyed, and those we may need to review.

Secondary Posts (100 words each for at least two or more classmates)

As for the secondary post, try to see the point of your peer, as you will be exploring multiple perspectives throughout this semester. Whereas, some of the points-of-view you may agree with, and yet others you may not agree at all. Remember to engage at least two or more peers in the discussion board. Welcome back. See you in class.

Writing Requirements

- Initial post length: 150–200 words
  - Due by Friday at 11:59 p.m.
- Secondary post length: Minimum of 100 words per post (respond to at least two classmates)
  - Due by Sunday at 11:59 p.m.

**Grading is 0% if no submission, or 5% on submission (5 points) – correct criterion will earn 5 points

Assignment – Critical Response In-Class Assignment

As you are attending college courses, making friends, developing networks, establishing social groups, enhancing your "parents" social standing, and learning your way through expectations, tasks, deadlines, collaboration, assimilation, attaining knowledge, and using it. When does college not matter anymore? As the friends you make in college, tend to be the people you stay the closest.

Based on the group activity, we are going to write a critical response to the notion of "college," as an institution, social standing, "right," and privilege. For example, Atwan (2014) states, "Education: Does College Still Matter? Delbanco (2012) challenges the reader to rethink the "American Dream" as higher education should focus more on specific careers and tasks, rather than encompassing multiple areas of study, especially from the "arts and sciences."

Reflect; as you read the titles did you know you would be discussing whether everyone has the right to attend college? First, in class we read the stories for this week, please try to activate your background knowledge on the subject or topic as you discover the "heading" such as the word college. Finally after reading, write a critical response on the topic, you will stick solely to the facts, whereas your opinion does not matter.

Please remember that you are developing an argument through your response, and that you are comfortable with in taking a position either for or against an author's intentionality. In other words, do you agree or disagree with the author's point-of-view? Do not use the words "agree," or "disagree."

For the Assignment (will take two class periods)

Please write 4–5 paragraphs (a basic essay) about "college." The first a summary of information you had from your background, such as you read the word college…were these mandates in the story all the same. Furthermore, in your group you have discussed several issues in the process. What have you learned? Next, the second step would be to focus on the topic, you will chose to write, and include the thesis statement. The third paragraph will be the "how to" implement your knowledge on the topic into a reflective essay based on the information you have acquired through the reading. The fourth will give details of the position you have taken for the topic. The final paragraph will be the conclusion.

Present the argument you intend to use as you are writing your academic research. In addition, remember to use in-text citation for any material discussed within the sample, as you will need at least two quotations, and two paraphrases from the readings. Please remember to support your work with in-text citations, and proper APA format.

Caveat

*Remember if it helps to create an outline first; please do it. Keep in mind there is a reference guide found in this chapter to show other brainstorming strategies. So, please use them, as these are other strategies to use in place of an outline, please remember to use at least one to create a type of prewriting strategy as your guide to finalize your writing sample. This will help you become a better writer.

Assessment and Grading

Upload Work to the Appropriate Area**

Writing Requirements (APA format)

- 1 page (approx. 300 words per page)
- 1-inch margins
- Double-spaced
- 12-point Times New Roman font
- Cover page
- Reference page (readings are the source)
- **Due date: In-Class Assignment**

**Grading is 0% if no submission, else 15% on submission (15 points) – correct criterion will earn 15 points

Charts and Diagrams (at times used interchangeably)

Charts are a way to give the reader an image of the necessary information used to collect data. In addition, the charts depending on their usage become an interactive tool to provide extension to the original context of a reading. Charts help in separating data, typically seen as a pie chart divided into sectors, or a bar graph divided with staggering bars, and line charts divided usually by horizontal lines to represent data, but charts are able to be represented in many shapes and sizes. Please refer the two pie charts and notice the variations in both forms.

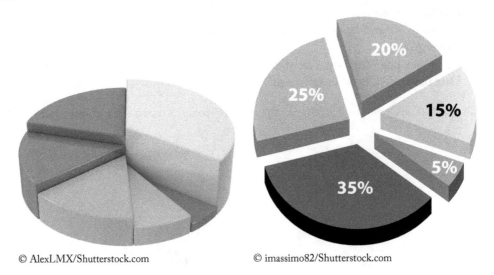

© AlexLMX/Shutterstock.com   © imassimo82/Shutterstock.com

Diagrams, just as charts, will give the reader an image of the necessary information utilized to collect data; however, diagrams use depending on the type of data you would like to collect. As there is both discrete data and continuous data, it will help to know the difference of data sets. Continuous data could take any value within a particular range (measurement), and discrete data should not contain information between two categories, such as 2 years, animals, cities, and the like. Types of diagrams could reflect, but are not limited to the following "histogram, pictogram, scattergram, or scatter plot."

Example of a Venn Diagram

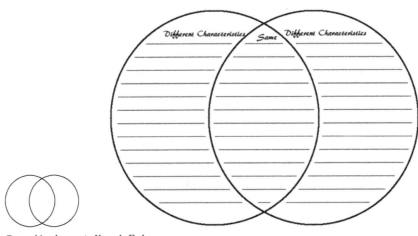

Created by Anastasia Krueck-Frahn

Lists

Lists are another way to organize data, generate ideas, create tasks, and develop strategies to recall information in a quick and logical manner, as the information is in "one place." Lists tend to create a feeling of accomplishment. As the task is finished, the item is "crossed off the list." A list as a tool in writing, time management, and goal setting will follow similar rules for both creating and revising. As the task is accomplished, it is removed or revised for further use at a later date.

© Cozine/Shutterstock.com

© Faberr Ink/Shutterstock.com

Clusters

Clustering might be considered as a "diagram" since it is another way to think of new ideas. The word "cluster" means a group of similar things. Clustering means words put into groups. Each group, or cluster, has a number of words that are related to each other. Clustering is similar to brainstorming. You try to think of many words and phrases. As you write the words and phrases in groups, there should be a connection from one thought to the next, as each represents topic, subtopics, or main idea, supporting details.

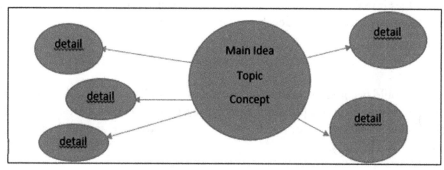

Created by Anastasia Krueck-Frahn

Simple Steps on How to Make a Cluster Map (process):

First, draw a large circle on the paper and center it.

Next, writing the topic inside the circle (main idea or claim).

Then make extensions, and draw and create smaller circles for major support (general ideas).

Finally, more extensions, and then extend off the major support to create minor support (fillers).

Lastly, continue the process until the main idea or claim is fully supported and there are no more ideas.

Assignment – Educational Autobiography

Writing an educational autobiography: We have the ability to connect ourselves on many levels, and in turn, we have the ability to reflect on our personal experiences to the social, political, or cultural meaning of education. This assignment is meant to provide a guide of your **educational experiences** throughout your lifetime. The issue will not be if you are a good storyteller. The challenge will be if you are able to tell the story of your life and base it on actual social issues in education.

As a point of reference, please try to remember any "autobiographies" you may have read. The person referenced, typically around their experiences in life, keep in mind, wrote the autobiography. For instance, the "Diary of Anne Frank" is often regarded as an autobiography. An educational autobiography will be a reflection on your personal educational events and link them to a larger social context. For example, we would share an educational event that left an impact on your life in a profound and meaningful way, such as becoming the "first generation college student," and being an athlete created the life-changing experience.

Purpose

The idea for having us reflect is to connect one of our own experiences, personal events, social exposures, while acknowledging the educational event that had impacted our life; in fact, the more apparent the significance to the event is revealed in your writing sample, the likelihood the reader will make a personal connection to your writing sample. Remember, as you write, keep in mind the audience, as each come from an eclectic array of diversity; it is easy to create bias in writing. A good way to keep this purpose organized is the use of chronological order, or time order as the event unfolds.

Criteria

Things to consider, is it a good story? Does the story have relevant meaning to education? Do you connect to a big picture? Does it make a connection to a social, political, or cultural issue? Does your experience explore or raise "new issues" coming or developing in our current society?

Audience

Remember anyone could become the reader, and there is a possibility these could lead to your first "peer review." As you are writing from one point-of-view, it is easy to create bias. Particularly, as bias is a "one-sided view, it could be either negative or positive in outlook." In writing, we should at least acknowledge there is another side to the story.

How to Develop

Title

The connection of your writing sample and the title we give to it should be a mirror of one another; for example, "Dogs on the Mississippi," as you read the title you would hope to read about dogs, and something about the Mississippi River. However, as we began to read the piece, the reader discovers "Mississippi" is the name of a street in Little Rock, Arkansas. As a second misguided piece, the writer was using "slang for men" calling those dogs. As this writing sample reflects around you and your educational experience, it will be good practice to make the title as "true" to the story, as the reader should have as little interpretation of you, as possible.

Narrative

In your youth, an elementary teacher would read the class stories, and the stories had "someone telling the story in the book." However, in this scenario, you are the narrator and your main purpose is more or less to "show and tell." As we write narratives, we want to include as much detail and support for the event to create a "big picture," as the use of adjectives will produce stronger images for the reader. Read the following… "Jack and Jill went up the hill," and now read "Jack, a virile young man, and his younger sibling Jill crossed the rocky terrain, as they climbed a steep never-ending hill full of brush, twigs, and large tree roots." The second sentence truly gave a clearer picture, although if you had the background knowledge for the "hill, Jack, or Jill" the image could still be different from the original intention of the author.

Remember, one of the hardest parts of this assignment will be to connect it to a social, political, or cultural issue. In addition, please make a personal connection and link it to a "bigger issue." As a suggestion, refer anything "pop culture" and use some of those issues to help develop your writing sample. You may have made a connection, as you were reading.

Issues to Consider

There are many, as these are just a small sample to explore…gender, private education, public education, socioeconomic standing, family life, extended family, sports, rote learning, authentic learning, boredom, engagement, and friendships.

Connections

In academic writing, it is important to make as many connections to the ideas of others, and use their knowledge to help support your own perspective. Once you have generated a core event and put it into a narrative, identify the "conceptual pattern that links it to a larger social context." Integrate the reading, as this will help develop the "analytical aspect" of the assignment. Remember, it is one thing to "tell a story," and another to show the reader the context in a theoretical perspective, as to see it as a "bigger" piece of your life. Lastly, you have to convince the reader, yes this event change my life, and if I did not make the difference in my life, who or what would?

Conclusion

As we conclude our thoughts, the writing sample should show a final connection to the opening paragraph, the support in the middle, and finally the end matches with the throughout your work. Your final thought must leave the reader with very little thought to your original intention of the work. In addition, as you conclude your final words and your argument, the reader's interpretation should match your point-of-view, even if they disagree with your position on a topic.

Remember as you do transition into your final thoughts, try to eliminate the words, "in conclusion, my conclusion, in my conclusion," whereas these are known to the reader as it is the end of your thoughts, and typically the last two paragraphs; therefore, you should have a conclusion. The use of transitional words, such as finally, particularly, lastly, furthermore, at last, this will give the reader clues you are about to end your writing sample.

Assessment and Grading

Writing Requirements (APA format)

- 1 pages (approx. 300 words per page)
- 1-inch margins
- Double-spaced
- 12-point Times New Roman font
- Cover page
- Reference page
- Due date: Sunday before 11:59 p.m.

**Grading is 0% if no submission, or is 10% on submission – the correct criterion will earn 10 points

Chapter 9

Integration of Media

Media

What is the Definition of Media?

According to Merriam-Webster, media is the means of "mass communication (especially television, radio, newspapers, and the Internet) regarded collectively. Oddly enough, the synonyms used to represent media as they are considered "the same" would be the press, the news, and the papers. As the media gathers information, collects data, compiles research, reports findings, draws conclusions, and predicts outcomes, we really do not have much to worry about as a society. Do we have any concerns to be misinformed, or misguided?

Social Media

What Defines the Media as Social?

According to Merriam-Webster, "social media" is defined as "websites and applications that enable users to create and share content or to participate in social networking." Whereas, the use of discussion boards, in the technical sense, would be considered "social media." However, if we did a quick survey of classmates, the answers that would repeat are more likely than not "Facebook, Twitter, Instagram, Snap Chat," and possibly "Myspace" as it is making a comeback to the 21st century. As everyone is connecting to "everyone else," the world seems to be "getting smaller," and the information technologies appear to be reporting information faster than the average person could retrieve it. Maybe, you have heard this familiar phrase: "I saw it on Facebook, it has to be true, right?" As the validity and reliability of the "social" tends to be at times furthest from the truth, where do we turn to find out, as I do not want to pass misinformation, or false information to someone I know, as they will do the same. As there are websites "combating truth," still misinformation is received minute-by-minute, hour-by-hour, and day-by-day. Next time you "see" something on a social media site, check the source try Snoops. A team of researchers will "find the answer."

Media Exploited

As our readings create an Informative Synthesis that directly cross-examines the use of media and social media in particular, whereas, Ghuman (2012) will focus on the issue of "Is Technology Destroying our Social Bonds?" He stated, "Over the past decade, social media has developed into a style of communication fit for our generation." Whose generation? Consequently, withstanding the "test of time," hence the media expressing "public opinion" for the greater good of our American society.

Furthermore, Atwan (2013) "The Persuasive Writer" uses "The Visual Expression of Opinions" to guide the reader to critically think through their eyes as they view a photograph, or "photography, political cartoons, and opinion advertisements," as they may not appear to express an opinion. Through the closer examination of placement, "role of context," iconography represents an immediate suggestion of incident, idea, etc., as this is critically thought as the same category of our English term of onomatopoeia. It literally means from Greek translation, "name I make" – as the word represents the sound, voice, name, and others (boom, bang, and screech). Particularly, as the majority of people look at a photograph as "just a picture, or memory," Atwan (2014) examines the illustrative purpose of imagery, as the "exaggeration, irony, caricature, symbol and caption" begin to take on "new meaning."

Besides, the image is literally the subject; however, the contrast of "what appears to be expressed, and what is actually expressed" might just be different. We may want to look twice at those images. Things are not always clear the first time we approach them. Especially, at first glance, just like visual literacy, not everything as it appears. The perspective or view may be missing an important vantage point.

"Mocking Birds" Chuck Wimmer (printed with permission)

Discussion 1

Process

The process of something is very important, especially in taking the proper steps in creating a final product. Therefore, the details must be clear, and the steps in some type should be of logical order. Remember, just because you are aware of the requirements does not mean you conveyed them properly.

Initial Post (150 words)

For this discussion, you are going to write down the steps for creating a peanut butter and jelly sandwich. Please review the guidelines to developing a "process." A process must have steps. Good luck.

Secondary Posts (100 words each with at least two or more classmates)

Please, look at your peer's work. Did they get it correct? If not, please help them, as making a sandwich appears to require more steps than others since, you may have seen as they developed the process. Remember to re-state part of their original discussion, as you modify the post. If you have any questions or concerns, please email me. See you in class.

Writing Requirements

- Initial post length: 150–200 words
  - Due by Tuesday at 11:59 p.m.
- Secondary post length: Minimum of 100 words per post (respond to at least two classmates)
  - Due by Sunday at 11:59 p.m.

**Grading is 0% if no submission, else 10% on submission (10 points) – correct criterion will earn 10 points

(Please note: this exercise will be modeled in our class, and random posts will be used as examples)

Assignment – Critique (Review)

For this assignment, we will be "critiquing the critique of another," as we will examine the use of the "interpretation based on the original work," and determine if the "critique" was fairly written. Furthermore, as critiques tend to show bias, the writing sample was developed without bias, prejudice, or cultural identification in text. As you read Ghuman (2013), "Peer Critique: Student Essay," review key topics that will lead to the "steps" in writing a critique of literature. Please examine one or two key issues that are addressed in the piece to help you write your critique.

As you move from the first draft through the revision and editing process to the final draft, focus first on big picture issues or global perspective. Does your essay make a point (argument) about the term you have coined? Do you support that point (argument) with specific details (evidence)? Have you organized your essay in a way that makes it easy for someone who has not spent nearly as much time working on this (thinking, reading, and writing) as you have? As stated these are some of the basic questions that all writers must wrestle with, as they revise their texts. Use the feedback you received from your peers, instructor, tutors, and friends as you move forward. Please review the guidelines for writing a critique.

What is a Critique?

A critique is a paper that gives a critical assessment of a book or article or other multimodal pieces.

Steps

Begin by reading the book or article and annotate as you read.

- Note the author's main point/thesis statement.
- Divide the book/article into sections of thought and write a brief summary of each thought in your own words.

Introduction

Start your critique with sentences giving the following information:

- Author's name
- Book/Article title and source
- Author's thesis statement

Summary

Summarize the author's purpose and main points/evidence cited that are used for back up, and make sure your work contains the author's name, year, and title of their work.

Review and Evaluate

Evaluation of the piece, the author's credibility, the logic, and your interpretation are critical.

To critically review the piece, ask the following questions:

- What are the credentials/areas of expertise of the author?
- Did the author use appropriate methods to gather the evidence?
- Did the author accurately use the evidence?
- Does the author's use and interpretation of this evidence lead the reader to the same conclusion?

- Did the author build a logical argument?
- Is there other evidence that would support a counter-argument?
- Are the article and the evidence still valid or are they outdated, leading to an invalid conclusion?
- Was the author successful in making his/her point?

Conclusion

Wrap up by:

- Stating whether you agree with the author.
- Backup your decisions by stating your reasons.
- Give a general opinion of the work.

Assessment and Grading

Upload Work to the Appropriate Area**

Writing Requirements (APA format)

- 2 pages (approximately 300 words per page)
- 1-inch margins
- Double-spaced
- 12-point Times New Roman font
- Cover page
- Reference page (as the reading is the source – please use in-text citations, and one Ohiolink source for support)
- Due date: Friday before 11:59 p.m.

**Grading is 0% if no submission, or 25% on submission – correct criterion will earn 25 points

Genre

As we look at paintings, listen to music, read poetry, open a novel, glance at a billboard, we are referencing "genre." A genre could be any type of literary work with a distinct purpose. As defined by Merriam-Webster, genre is a "category or class of artistic endeavor having a particular form, content, technique, or the like: genus, kind, sort, or style." For instance, the genre of improvisation as "jazz" will be a style of its own.

Through the integration of media, genre plays a key role in the multiperspective of opinion, visual (eyes) interpretation, auditory (hearing) interpretation, olfactory (smell) interpretation, kinesthetic (touch), and savor (taste) of a palatable object. Likewise, as we research topics we develop a multigenre perspective; therefore, a multigenre essay is developed into a "bigger picture," or a well-rounded view of a topic. Literally, "the sky is the limit" to produce a multigenre piece.

Have a quick glance at snippets of a multigenre piece personally created many years ago. See if you are able to identify the following genre, as there may be research, case studies, poetry, reflection, imagery, and a possible review of literature. Whereas you may lack some relevant information to "guess correctly" for a few of the genres, the majority should be able to recognize at a glance. As you will see, there are a variety of genre collected throughout our page. For our discussions, assignments, and reading, we will focus on the use of multiple genre.

Below is a brief list and an example of a **Multigenre Paper (personally created in academics)**

A Brief List of Genres:

- Journal Entries
- Personal Letter
- Greeting Card
- Schedule/Things to Do List
- Inner Monolog Representing Internal Conflicts
- Classified or Personal Ads
- Personal Essay or Philosophical Questions
- Top Ten List/Glossary or Dictionary
- Poetry
- Song Lyrics
- Autobiographical Essay
- Contest Entry Application
- Business Letter or Correspondence/Persuasive or Advocacy Letter
- Biographical Summary
- Critique of a Published Source
- Speech or Debate
- Historical Times Context Essay
- Textbook Article
- Science Article or Report/Business Article or Report
- Lesson Plan
- Encyclopedia Article
- Short Scene from a Play with Notes for Stage Directions
- Short Scene from a Movie with Notes for Camera Shots

- Dialogue of a Conversation among Two or More People
- Short Story
- Adventure Magazine Story
- Ghost Story
- Myth, Tall Tale, or Fairy Tale
- Talk Show Interview or Panel
- Recipe and Description of Traditional Holiday Events
- Classroom Discussion
- Character Analysis or Case Study
- Comedy Routine or Parody
- Liner Notes
- Picture Book
- Chart or Diagram with Explanation and Analysis
- Brochure or Newsletter
- Time Line or Chain of Events
- Map with Explanation and Analysis
- Magazine or TV Advertisement or Infomercial
- Restaurant Description and Menu
- Travel Brochure Description
- How-To or Directions Booklet
- Receipts, Applications, Deeds, Budgets, or Other Documents
- Wedding, Graduation, or Special Event Invitation
- Birth Certificate
- Local News Report
- Pop-Up Book
- Review and Poster for a Movie, Book, or TV Program
- Board Game or Trivial Pursuit with Answers and Rules
- Comic Strip or Graphic Novel Excerpt
- Power Point Presentation
- Informational Video
- Web Site
- Future News Story
- Letter to the Editor
- Newspaper or Magazine Feature/Human Interest Story
- Obituary, Eulogy, or Tribute
- News Program Story or Announcement
- Tabloid Article

Example of a Multigenre Paper

Let Us Read

Research – "Reading and Writing: A Winning Combination, Let's Play" Krueck-Frahn (2004)

Language development is also a natural process in children's developmental years. Play and language are viewed as primary ways for children to learn. The psychological and sociological well-being of children is enhanced through the value of play. Play creates the environment for which children's behaviors would enhance language and literacy development for years to come (Krueck-Frahn, 2004).

Fairy Tale: *"Faraway"*

Once upon a time, there was a king and a queen. They lived in a faraway place. There was no fighting, no guns, and most of all no hunger. The children of Faraway could play safely. They had no fear, and knew there was little danger. The children could wake up, eat their breakfast, and go outside to play. They could play all day. They played simple games such as kick the can, or kick ball (Krueck-Frahn, 2004).

"Public Address"

Legislators would have the public believe that children need more time spent in academic preparation. School districts have labeled the time to play in school as "recess," which meant that the time for play in school would be outside allowing a few minutes of play during the children's lunch break.

Problem: Concern: Issue

The problem was that children were not being given breaks throughout the day, to ensure more learning time. The children were being drilled, tested, and assessed without time throughout the day to absorb the information being taught.

Letter to the Editor:

"Give Children a Break"

Doctor's take a break; lawyers take a break, judges schedule recesses, educators take a break, plumbers. The fact is that most occupations take into consideration that we need a break. Do our children take breaks? The city of Toledo was recognized as a city in 1837. The original doctrine establishing rules and regulations contained "Articles." Article 10 states the following, "each scholar (child) is entitled to 15 minutes in the morning and 15 minutes in the afternoon." This is a sign of the times, and we have certainly regressed. Studies show for successful development that a child needs to have a form of recess.

Created by Anastasia Krueck-Frahn

Discussion 2

Process of a Critique

For this discussion, we will be "critiquing the critique of another," as we will examine the use of the "interpretation based on the original work," and determine if the "critique" was fairly written. As you had the opportunity to read the original work as well, did the student writer provide enough background information about the reading, before you ever read it?

Consequently, there are many questions to consider in critiquing the critique of another, and information will play the major role. First consider the following, did they identify the author, and give the year the piece was published? Was there a brief summary of the work? Were there enough details to support their perspective? Now, something else to consider, what if they got it wrong? How do you know they got it right? Where is your proof?

Initial Post (150 words)

For your initial post reflect on the Critique Review. Create a description of your process, as you recall the first items you looked for in the review of the literature. Second, reflect on the ease of the assignment; reviewing someone else looking at a reading, developing an interpretation, and then writing it. Finally, review the literature yourself and create a writing sample with your interpretation. Lastly, compare the two interpretations against the original work. Did you properly cite your work?

Furthermore, if you felt the review of someone else as they interpreted a reading gave you another perspective that you may not have had by just reading the piece, explain why, and the difference between your thoughts and that of another. If you felt you were better off just reading the work for yourself, explain why and the difference. Remember to always support your work with at least one quote and one paraphrase with proper in-text citation.

Secondary Posts (100 words each with at least two or more classmates)

As you begin your secondary post, please find at least two classmates that "do not see it your way." For the sake of argument, please remember to re-state their perspective, and as the rebuttal steer your classmate to "your side." Remember to keep all discussion posts positive, as this is a skill in developing critical thought. If you have any questions or concerns, please email me.

Writing Requirements

- Initial post length: 150–200 words
  - Due by Friday at 11:59 p.m.
- Secondary post length: Minimum of 100 words per post (respond to at least two classmates)
  - Due by Sunday at 11:59 p.m.

**Grading is 0% if no submission, else 10% on submission (10points) – correct criterion will earn 10 points

Assignment – Multigenre Paper

For this assignment, we will be "multigenre essay or multigenre paper," as we will examine the use of the "interpretation based on the original work," and determine multiple ways to produce fairly a well-written work of our own. Furthermore, as our writing sample will come from only one perspective; however, we must be careful as not to show bias, and become cognizant that our writing sample should be developed without prejudice, or cultural identification. Our text should reflect a much higher order of thought.

Nevertheless, in a review of the "multigenre," it has been copied directly to the assignment for your perusal. Remember to pick a variety of genre to represent your theme, main idea, topic, issue, or concern in literature. The majority work is your creation; however, remember to give credit for ideas copied and presented in your writing sample to avoid plagiarism.

Genre

As we look at paintings, listen to music, read poetry, open a novel, glance at a billboard, we are referencing "genre." A genre could be any type of literary work with a distinct purpose. As defined by Merriam-Webster, genre is a "category or class of artistic endeavor having a particular form, content, technique, or the like: genus, kind, sort or style." For instance, the genre of improvisation as "jazz" will be a style of its own.

Through the integration of media, genre plays a key role in the multiperspective of opinion, visual (eyes) interpretation, auditory (hearing) interpretation, olfactory (smell) interpretation, kinesthetic (touch), and savor (taste) of a palatable object. Likewise, as we research topics we develop a multigenre perspective; therefore, a multigenre essay is developed into a "bigger picture," or a well-rounded view of a topic. Literally, "the sky is the limit" to produce a multigenre piece. Be creative.

For example, the topic – social misrepresentation

The first genre you chose was poetry (genre)…you begin the piece "I wish I was a computer." The second an image (genre) of a computer with multiple "windows" open. The third piece gives the history (genre) of computer technology. The fourth piece reflects a movie (genre) "Aliens." Finally, the fifth was a piece of music (genre) that depicted a glitch in a computer program.

Requirements

The focus of our readings tend to imply the implications of media and social media. Please chose a genre that will support a topic to depict accurately your point-of-view. There will be a minimum of five different genres presented to represent your overall "idea." Topics of interest could be social stereotyping, relationships, family, responsibility, technology, opinions of the media, visual expression, social bonds, research, loss, gain, editorials, and there are many others…these are just a few.

Rubric (guide)

The essay must reflect formal and informal writing, have no less than five different genre styles throughout your work (must be identifiable), transition between pieces smooth and fluent (genre, such as an explanation (text), may be needed to go from one piece to the next), topic must be identifiable, and length should be no less than 2–3 pages.

Assessment and Grading

Upload Work to the Appropriate Area**

Writing Requirements (APA format)

2–3 pages (approx. 300 words per page)

- 1-inch margins
- Double-spaced
- 12-point Times New Roman font
- Cover page
- Reference page
- Due date: Sunday before 11:59 p.m.

**Grading is 0% if no submission, or 25% on submission (25 points) – correct criterion will earn 25 points

Chapter 10

Movie Project/Research Paper

Another Critique: How to Write a Movie Review – Media

Watch the Movie

Consequently, one of the first steps in writing the review is to watch the movie. Watch the movie in a relaxed environment that is familiar to you, and you are able to possibly stop and watch more than once. You do not want to be distracted by an unfamiliar room. Remember, watching the movie a second time will help you absorb a lot more detail about the movie. Most movie reviewers take notes as they watch the movie review.

Evaluate the Movie

Evaluating the movie will require some of your opinion, therefore be careful as to eliminate bias in the writing sample. Whereas, you will need to evaluate the notion of multiple perspectives into the discussion area, try not to create stereotyping, culture bias, or religious undertones. Most movie reviewers will give their opinion of the movie. Importantly, you are the reviewer, which means you are able to express the elements of the movie, either as having been enjoyed or having been lamented in nature. Nevertheless, as in all good journalism, the reviewer should always produce impartial details, which should allow the reader to make their own mind, particularly, as an issue the reader may have liked or disliked, as they too have watched the same film.

This is Your Recommendation "Who is Your Audience?"

You need to consider the audience. Remember that as you are writing a movie review for children, this will require a different approach than writing for a movie club. Ensure you report on the factors that matter to your likely audience. For example, this movie was rated PG-13; however, I felt as an adult the content should have had a stronger rating, such as Rated-R.

Give an Outline or Overview

Give the outline of the movie, but do not give away essential details such as the end or any surprises, whereas you would like the audience to enjoy the movie in its entirety, without ruining the movie. Consequently, if there is a twist or "big surprise," you want to entice the reader by dropping clues, or establishing suspense, this will just give the hint something special, big, or out of the ordinary might happen. Please do not give away the "what."

Questions to Prompt a "Good Review"

Actors

If the movie may contain actors, as most do, show details to the main (character) star in the movie and if they acted well. Second, any supporting actors – did they do their job in giving the main character (star) support? For example, Julia Roberts in the film "Pretty Woman," did she do a believable character?

Structure

Did the movie follow a regular predictable story line, or did it get you thinking? Did the movie predict revelation?

Cinematography and Lighting

Give details about how well the movie was shot and directed. Was the lighting good in the setting the mood for the scenes? Lighting used in creating suspense? Cinematography and lighting used in establishing diversion among the characters?

Music

Did the movie have its own score, similar to the one used in Amadeus Mozart, or ET, or did it feature songs from popular artists?

Snippets

Did the movie have "footage" after either it ended, or this footage could be the very last image seen by the "movie goer," or precedes the initial post of credits for the movie?

Research/Take a Trip to the Library

Conducting Basic Research for an Essay or Project

Why do some people research anything? Simple, they need to validate information, learn, expand on a topic, write a paper, "find support," or possibly just intrigued by learning new things. For our course, we need to learn all of the above and then some. Remember this is practice.

How to Use the Ohiolink

1. Search the University's Library Source via their online portal
2. Please sign in – permission to access the site; for example, a bar code or student ID
3. Select – Library Resources
4. Type your topic in the search box and hit enter (i.e., "Smoking" "Pop Culture" "Friends")
5. How many items are listed? _____Print the page showing the number of results.
6. Limit the number of results by adding an additional search term to your original query; for example, "Smoking and teenagers." How many results are listed now? _____
7. Now limit by the type of material. On the left-hand side, select the word **"books,"** and click update. How many **books** are listed? _____Print this page for reference.
8. Choose one of the **books** that appear on the page you have printed and click on the title. How many libraries own this book? _____Does your university have this book on campus? Yes or No. If yes, is the book available for you to check it out? How do you check out a book at our library? _____ Where is our library located? _____ _____What are the hours? _____
9. If you want a printed copy of the book, you may choose to check it out, please make sure you have the correct data for the Reference Librarian. If they have to order the book from another institution, please give the location of the campus, reference number of the book, "title" of the book, author or authors, and the year of publication.
10. Now try the exercises one more time…try the search for "articles" on the same topic…you will repeat the steps you have just completed with the books. However, please know there are several types of articles – journals, periodicals, magazines, newspapers, tradebooks, and other academic sources.

Remember as technology has increased the need for electronic media, please know that PDF files, html files, and eSources are available for academic references as well. Please make sure that your information is current, and typically no older than 10 years back from the current year.

Discussion

Movie Review – Movie to be Shown in Class

For the purpose of writing a "movie review," you will become the main critic; therefore, it is imperative that you include the following information in your critique to establish enough background information to the audience. You will need to write a plot summary for the movie. Consequently, most movie (film) reviews are designed to be a guide for a particular genre, whether it has the focus of comedy, horror, drama, documentary, sci-fi, or any number of movie categories.

Similar to writing any review, you should analyze the effectiveness of the overall movie first; in other words, did the movie leave an indelible impression, or was the movie awful enough to create disdain. Next, analyze the elements, similar to a book, such as the character development (acting), the antagonist (the "bad guy"), protagonist (the "good guy"). Furthermore, the plot, "time-period," costumes, underlying theme, direction, special effects, setting, cinematography, mating, originality, musical effects, and many other elements create a movie. Lastly, you are to make a comparison based on adaptation; particularly, if the movie was based on a novel, short story, play texts, film scripts, pop culture, "real-life" (biography, autobiography), or historical, technological, journalistic, futuristic, or broader culture.

Specifically, there are qualities and guidelines that a critique of a movie should possess in your writing sample. Conversely, avoid, eliminate, and curtail overgeneralizations as you state your opinions; for example, "Oh, it was a great movie," or "that was the worst acting I have ever seen." Rather, give very specific points of the movie that were great, or the re-enactment of the "worst acting." Be sure to give specific reasons and always include the "why." As a guideline, there is no limit to you words; however, the minimum should be no less than 150 words in the discussion boards, but this one will be slightly longer.

Finally, you will need to include the following: name of the movie (film/picture), prominent stars of the visual imaging, setting (time and place), and type of film (sci-fi, comedy, adventure, drama, etc.). Remember, you will need to write a plot summary for the movie. Do not reveal the ending. Concurrently, discuss at least five events and be sure to cover the entire scope of the movie, except the very end. Costumes suggest time, type of acting, choosing from any direction of the movie to the editing of the film. Look at the costume design (believable), set design, photography, background music, or anything else you may think of was relevant to the picture. Make sure to always use in-text citations to support the film, and be specific.

Suggestions for Comprising a Good Review – Use the following prompts and questions as a guide

Initial Post: (200–300 words)

Watch the Movie

Consequently, one of the initial steps in writing the review is to watch the movie. Watch the movie in a relaxed environment that is familiar to you, i.e., you are able to possibly stop and watch more than once. You do not want to be distracted by an unfamiliar room. Remember, watching the movie a second time will help you absorb a lot more detail about the movie. Most movie reviewers take notes as they watch the movie review.

Evaluate the Movie

Evaluating the movie will require some of your opinion, therefore be careful as to eliminate bias in the writing sample. Whereas you will need to evaluate the notion of multiple perspectives into the discussion area, try not to create stereotyping, culture bias, or religious undertones. Most movie reviewers will give their opinion of the movie. Importantly, you are the reviewer, which means you are able to express the elements of the movie, either as having been enjoyed or having been lamented in nature. Nevertheless, as in all good journalism, the reviewer should always produce impartial details, which should allow the reader to make their own mind; particularly, for an issue, the reader may have liked or disliked it, as they too have watched the same film.

This is Your Recommendation "Who is Your Audience?"

You need to consider the audience. Remember that as you are writing a movie review for children, this will require a different approach than writing for a movie club. Ensure you report on the factors that matter to your likely audience. For example, this movie was rate PG-13; however, I felt that as an adult the content should have had a stronger rating, such as Rated-R.

Give an Outline or Overview

Give the outline of the movie, but do not give away essential details such as the end or any surprises, since you would like the audience to enjoy the movie in its entirety, without ruining the movie. Consequently, if there is a twist or "big surprise," you want to entice the reader by dropping clues or establishing suspense; this will just give the hint something special, big, or out of the ordinary might happen. Please do not give away the "what."

Actors

Provide details, the main (character), the star in the movie, and if they acted well. Second, any supporting actors – did they do their job, as in giving the main character (star) support? For example, Julia Roberts in the film "Pretty Woman," did she do a believable character?

Structure

Review the "story line," was it predictable or did it get you thinking? Did the movie predict revelation? What was the angle the film was "shot in" or location in? Was the lighting considered good? Was the lighting poorly displayed throughout the film? What is Cinematography? Was the lighting good in setting the mood for the scenes? Is lighting used in creating suspense? Are cinematography and lighting used in establishing diversion among the characters?

Music

Did the movie have its own score, similar to the one used in Amadeus Mozart, or did the film use a popular artist, such as JLo or Ed Sheeren?.

Secondary Posts (100 words each post in the discussion area)

Must post to at least two or more classmates in the discussion board. Please review a couple of movie reviews that you read in the discussion board and reflect on the following questions as a guide to assist you formulate if the review could be valid.

1. Did your peer give enough background for you to visualize the movie?
2. Did your peer establish the criterion of characters, plot, or setting, and so on to entice you to possibly either view the movie or decide against this visual effects altogether?
3. Was the review from your peer able to guide you potentially watch the movie? If you would not ever watch the movie, was it based on the lack of recommendation? Were you left as the reader, which gave the impression you could not even understand the content of the film; therefore, Are you confused?
4. Did they write a good review?
5. Based on the review, was a recommendation included in the content?
6. If you have seen the movie, please give similarities and differences to your approach, interpretation, or overall recommendation either for or against the movie.
7. As in film and literature, please give a brief interpretation as to a movie that may be similar in nature to the one of your peer review. If you have not already seen the movie being described in their review. For example, the movies "E.T." and "Short-Circuit" both could be viewed as foreign entities, they are both around the same height, similar builds or structure, both have a sense of curiosity, and that they both "steel the heart" of the main character.

Writing Requirements

Please copy and paste your review into the proper designated area (Do not upload the document – this must be visible)

Due date:

- Initial post length: Minimum of 200–300 words
  Due by Friday at 11:59 p.m.
- Secondary post length: Minimum of 100 words per post (respond to at least two classmates)-due by Sunday at 11:59 p.m.

**Grading is 0% if no submission, or is 5% for submission (5 points) – correct criterion will earn 5 points

Assessment and Grading

Upload work to the appropriate area**

Writing requirements (APA format)

- 1 page (approx. 300 words per page)
- 1-inch margins
- Double-spaced
- 12-point Times New Roman font

**Grading is 0% no submission or is 25% submission– correct criterion will earn 25 points

Assignment – Movie Project/Research Paper

Issue in Media

Throughout your academic career, you will be asked to write papers in which you compare and contrast two things: two texts, two theories, two historical figures, two scientific processes, and so on. "Classic" compare-and-contrast papers, in which you weigh two pieces equally, may be about two similar things that have crucial differences (two pesticides with different effects on the environment) or two similar things that have crucial differences, yet turn out to have surprising commonalities (two politicians with vastly different worldviews who voice unexpectedly similar perspectives on college funding).

For this assignment, please refer our Lecture for information on "how to write a movie review," discussed in a collaborative engagement "what" was a "good movie review?" Finally, we will write an essay that will focus on one global issue presented in the movie. For example, as the movie develops the characters and plot, the issue of "friendship" appears, where do the characters go wrong? True friendships withstand the "hands of time," does the story depict realization through iconology, or the personification reflects actual dissonance among "people?"

As you begin your rough draft, basic research you have found on your topic and you will then use a compare or contrast writing style. You will write a draft on which you have made a connection, which you may choose from one of the readings. If you choose to outsource, remember, as you have done in class, we learned "how to" use the Ohiolink. Please remember that you will need two resources for your draft, as you will be supporting the "issue" from the movie you watched in class.

The Ohiolink research is the material that you will use in writing the rough draft, which will later become the final draft. Remember that in each research piece you must be able to use the in-text citation from the material in order to make a clear connection to your thoughts on a specific topic in pop culture. Being able to represent the ideas of others responsibly in your own writing is an important skill for academic writers.

Requirements

Write formal comparative paper

One topic (personal experience)

Compare Movie to Experience or Contrast Movie to Experience

This project consists of comprising your background knowledge with two viable sources of reference material. The reference material maybe, but not limited to an Academic Journal; Academic Articles; newspaper current events; valid internet resources (Wikipedia may not be used); movie; textbook. Please refer the syllabus for cross-curricular material to compare the movie with textbook findings. ***Please cite all materials that will be included in your project.***

1. **Topic:** must be a comparative form of information utilized within context.
2. **Standard writing format:** Well-developed ideals, global (general) topic, clear thesis statement, support, evidence, clearly stated position on the topic, and conclusive evidence to support your position.

3. Paper must be 3–5 pages in length (1500–2500 words).
4. **Set-up consists:** 12-point font, double-spaced.
5. Times New Roman, APA standard format.
6. **In-text** citation to the research used in your work – two viable sources.
7. (APA – **owl.english.purdue.edu/owl/resource/560/01**)
8. **Format** must follow the guidelines accurately to avoid plagiarism.
9. **Heading** or **Title** on paper must reflect content.
10. The paper will focus on persuasion, argument, or compare/contrast.
11. Topic sentence must be clear and conclusion must reflect topic.
12. Thesis statement must include all areas of concern for the given topic and must be conclusive in nature to be re-stated in final analysis of paper.
13. Reference page or work cite must be attached to paper.
14. Title page and work cited/reference page (not counted in total pages).
15. Project will take one week – due date: TBA in class.

TIMELINE: Project will be completed in a timely manner. The topic must reflect material presented in movie and/or textbook. A comparative summarization of all material must be included in the final paper. Suggestions to follow standard writing format – for example, brainstorm, outline, draft, revision, proofread, listing of all major support, verify source, in-text citation must be utilized to avoid plagiarism. Please use a dictionary for correct spelling and pronunciations of words, spell checker and grammarly.com or relevant grammar program found in "Word." Remember to read your work aloud for clarity, read your work backwards, and if you have any questions or concerns, please email me.

Assessment and Grading

Upload Work to the Appropriate Area**

Writing Requirements (APA format) – Rough Draft

- 3–5 pages (1500–2500 words)
- 1-inch margins
- Double-spaced
- 12-point Times New Roman font
- Cover page
- Reference page (2 must be correctly placed)
- Due date: Sunday before 11:59 p.m.

**Grading is 0% if no submission, else 50% on submission – correct criterion will earn 50 points

Plagiarism

Consequently, as we are closing fast on the end of the semester, by now, the proper use of references has been applied to everything you will do in academics, whether essays, discussion, informal writing, or formal writing. If you "get" the knowledge from another source, even if you had prior knowledge, "your mind is tainted," and you must give credit, "where credit is due."

Keep in mind that you must provide a reference for any work that you read, view, hear, touch, or taste; therefore, if you use it, the in-text citations must be presented in your posts, and if the reference of the same page represents both the "quotes" and paraphrases, please list the reference at the end of the paragraph. Please reference the following examples of eliminating plagiarism within our writing samples.

First, I am going to show you some different formats for Frost (1876), which are fictitious for the citation within the text or the in-text citations, and this will help you finish this class, and many other courses in college.

Paraphrase

Along time ago, Abraham Lincoln in 1859 decided that a change was needed in the America's; whereas his campaign changed the American way of life (Frost, 1876).

Paraphrase and Quote

Lincoln "spoke," another wrote the article.

According to George C Frost, a long time ago, Abraham Lincoln in 1859 decided that a change was needed in the America's; whereas, Frost (1876) stated, Lincoln's campaign changed the American way of life, as the "House Divided" speech emerged and America listened to the ideals of a nation (p.4).

Quote

Finally, Frost (1876) stated, "the campaign that change America's history was Abraham Lincoln's notable train ride across the United States of America" (p.4).

At the same time, here is another example to help make the connection. You finally have a job and you are making good money at this job. In walks someone off the street and takes your check, cashes it and for now gets away with it. Oddly, you do not want someone taking your check, for your hard work; please do not "take the work of others."

"Is It Plagiarism, Yet?" Stolley, Brizee, and Paiz (2013) state scenarios and laws, along with lists and situations. Please reference any questions on format to Purdue OWL, or other resources you may have found in academics. Just don't do it!

Chapter 11

Review Text and Relation to Main Idea

Implicit versus Explicit Meaning

Explicit (Directly Stated, or Denotation)

Remember, reading has varied levels of understanding, and depending on the content will require readers to use staggered reading rates, especially for comprehension. Keep in mind, the first couple of paragraphs should grab the reader's attention. Therefore, the summary of a passage, along with the main idea will be presented to the reader. However, only if the main idea is explicit will the content be directly stated in the passage. A stated main idea is a topic sentence. Remember, the stated main idea is very specific within the writing sample.

For example, football players are required to wear helmets while playing the game. Again, the main idea "helmets" states the requirement, and is very specific, or directly stated in the sentence.

Once the main idea is located, posing it as a question will help locate the supporting details in a passage. Remember, a major supporting detail illustrates, develops, and directly explains the main idea. Minor supporting details illustrate, develop, or explain the major supporting detail, or supporting details found within the passage. In other words, a major detail is one that directly supports the main idea of the passage; in contrast, the minor detail supports or explains the major detail.

Implicit (Implied, or Connotation)

Unfortunately, there are hidden meanings throughout reading, as everything read clearly lacks a direct meaning within certain passages. Therefore, we must become skilled readers, and find the "topic" of an implied piece of work. As we will have to make an educated guess, or draw a hypothesis for a good solution, finding the controlling point will help identify the topic faster. In other words, looking for the one point given repeatedly, or even an opinion about the topic, will reveal details. Remember, a main idea that is not stated directly but is strongly suggested by the supporting details in a passage is the implied main idea. The "implicit thought" should be the one idea that is "not too general, nor too specific" within the writing sample.

For example, football is a rough sport, football players are injured on the field all of the time, and safety equipment should be a priority in the game. As "safety equipment" is a general topic, the types of details, suggestions, and thought pattern an author uses will develop a topic.

For Review

An **implicit** (implied) main idea is the main point suggested by the types of details and thought patterns an author used to develop a topic.

An **explicit** (stated) main idea is a topic sentence, which in turn states the topic and the author is controlling the point about that topic.

Discussion

For our discussion this week, topics discussed in our readings could be viewed as exaggerated, or even ironic. Ironically, could they be true? Hsu (2009) describes the "white American" as an identity viewed by minorities and immigrants in America, and supports the view by quoting sociologist Matt Wray, as stating "racial-identity crisis." As our American culture strives for change, we still "live within the structures of privilege, injustice and racial categorization." Whereas, diversity has many factors such as age, race, background, religion, socioeconomic standing, education, career, gender, lifestyle, heredity, and culture (p.153).

Initial Post (150–200 words)

As the "new cultural mainstream" becomes the norm, and reflects upon diversity, "and whose ultimate goal is some vague notion of racial transcendence, rather than subversion or assimilation." Do you agree with the "categorization" of "mainstream?" Why or why not? Remember to use a summary of the reading to develop background of the topic, and support your work with at least one direct quote and one paraphrase from Hsu (2009) "The End of White America."

Secondary Posts (100 words each with at least two or more classmates)

As you have read Hsu (2009) "The End of White America," were you shocked by the title. Take a moment to reflect on the following: "We saw something different…it was a bridge and we crossed it." As you engage with your peers or classmates original post, please decide if you agree with their interpretation or disagree with it. If you agree, add more support to their original post; remember to begin by re-stating a portion of the post. However, if you disagree you must provide at least three examples from Hsu (2009) that support your interpretation, again remember to re-state a portion of your peer's original post.

Writing Requirements

- Initial post length: 150–200 words
  o Due by Friday at 11:59 p.m.
- Secondary post length: Minimum of 100 words per post (respond to at least two classmates)
  o Due by Sunday at 11:59 p.m.

**Grading is 0% if no submission, else is 10% for submission (10 points) – correct criterion will earn 10 points

Text – What Does it Mean Anyway?

Author Intentionality (purpose)

Author intentionality has a fine line between the authors being an expert, trying to sell you a concept, deliver directions, or just convince you "they are right." In other words, "what is the author trying to do?" Collectively, an author can draw on inference, which is the unstated idea that suggests facts or details in a passage. We must again become a skilled reader to sort the facts from the opinions, to decide the author's meaning.

As many authors tend to write from one side, this creates the concept of "bias." Please keep in mind, a great writer eliminates bias from their writing sample. However, we tend to confuse bias and prejudice, whereas bias could be either positive or negative depending on the one view. Regardless, you are strongly suggested to eliminate bias from writing, as there are "at least two sides to every story."

Three Main Types of their "Purpose"

To inform (media) – As we review a textbook, we gather **information** to learn content, subject matter, or a new concept. This writer looks at a perspective from many sides, looks at an issue equally, and writes without any preference to the outcome. Keep in mind, the writer wants to inform their readers, explain, describe, or investigate something. Common uses for informative writing or for "inform" are recipe cards, instructions, process, newspaper articles, directions, and "how to books."

To persuade (sales) – As we argue for or against a topic, concept, or idea, create bias or even "celebrate or attack a person, place, or thing." Keep in mind, the writer needs you to see their side, and you must take the same position of the writer to be successful in **persuasion**. Common uses for persuasion are persuasive or argumentative essays, advertisements, advertisers, advertising, pamphlets, political campaigns, and typically associated with words or phrases that will create urgency, such as "need to," "limited," "should," "must," "have to," "best or lowest," and "once in a lifetime."

To entertain (emotion) – As we write different genres to confront emotion, recognize humor, discovering the impossible, sympathy, desire, romance, mystery, fear, and science fiction, we are creating some form of **entertainment**. Importantly, writers that want to entertain are striving to give you some type of enjoyment; for the same reason writers that want to entertain may focus on the enjoyment of "being scared." Hence, write horror novels, movies, and short stories.

Tone (attitude)

Understanding the writers' **tone** is trying to understand their attitude at the time they wrote their work. Unlike the oral language, the written language or rhetoric tends to be more complicated as to figure out exactly the "mood toward the subject." However, there is "help" as we pay close attention to the diction (word choices), the reader through reflection should be able to identify if the writer was angry, sad, depressed, lost, happy, excited, or other expressive language. For example, this candy is gross! This candy has fungus, and looks disgusting on the inside of the wrapper.

Irony (expects one thing and gets another)

Irony usually involves a situation that will happen with unexpected results, and the writer uses diction to create a clash of events, or will use the words to state the opposite of their precise meaning within the writing sample. Look at the following sentence. Today, looked like rain, as the dark clouds moved across the sky, the sun came out.

Exaggeration (told out of proportion)

As you think of **exaggeration** used in writing, re-visit your youth for this example. Probably someone was very good at telling a "tall-tale," or the "larger than life" rendition of an event. We may even know someone like that now. Exaggeration is the use of overstating a situation usually to an unbelievable proportion of the "true" event or story. For example, in our modern day, Western action movies, comedies, punches in film, hero takes on the villain (odds are unbelievable), or the story just lacks reality.

Literal versus Figurative Language

The author's choices and attempt to explain their significance – another way to look at an analysis – would be to place the event from your perspective. **Literal** means to reflect a "textbook definition" of a term. Whereas, **figurative** will use the "words beyond their original meaning, place them against terms with no commonality, and use it as though it were part of our colloquial language (everyday common speech). Remember, with all vocabulary, if you do not use it, the meaning may become lost over time.

Review of Literary Terms to Know for Reading Novels

Connotation – implied meanings

Denotation – words directly made in association with the meaning

Exaggeration – a statement or action that represents something as better or worse than it really is, or appears to be

Figurative – the use of words to express meaning beyond the literal

Hyperbole – exaggeration

Imagery – the author's attempt to create mental picture

Metaphor – contrasting two seemingly unalike things that have a common interest, and enhance the situation

Simile – contrasting two seemingly unalike things that have a common interest, to enhance the meaning of a situation or themes using "like or as."

Assignment – Movie Project/Research Paper Final Draft

Issue in Media

Now, you begin the final process to your "movie project," which was to write an essay that would compare and contrast two things: two texts, two theories, two historical figures, two scientific processes, and so on. "Classic" compare-and-contrast papers, in which you weigh two pieces equally, may be about two similar things that have crucial differences (two pesticides with different effects on the environment) or two similar things that have crucial differences, yet turn out to have surprising commonalities (two politicians with vastly different worldviews who voice unexpectedly have similar perspectives on college funding).

Remember, this assignment, as we have reviewed our lecture for information on "how to write a movie review," discussed in a collaborative engagement "what" was a "good movie review?" Finally, we will write an essay that will focus on one global issue presented in the movie. For example, as the movie develops the characters and plot, the issue of "friendship" appears, where do the characters go wrong?

Requirements

Write formal comparative paper (Final Draft)

One topic (personal experience)

Compare Movie to Experience or Contrast Movie to Experience

This project consists of comprising your background knowledge with two viable sources of reference material. The reference material maybe, but not limited to an Academic Journal; Academic Articles; newspaper current events; valid internet resources (Wikipedia may not be used); movie; textbook. Please refer the syllabus for cross-curricular material to compare the movie to textbook findings. *Please cite all material that will be included in your project.*

1. Topic – must be a comparative form of information utilized within context
2. Standard writing format – Well-developed ideals, global (general) topic, clear thesis statement, support, evidence, clearly stated position on the topic, and conclusive evidence to support your position
3. Paper must be 3–5 pages in length (1500–2500 words)
4. Set-up consists of 12-point font, double-spaced
5. Times New Roman, APA standard format
6. **In-text** citation to the research used in your work – two viable sources.
7. **(APA – owl.english.purdue.edu/owl/resource/560/01)**
8. **Format** must follow the guidelines accurately to avoid plagiarism
9. **Heading** or **Title** on paper must reflect content
10. The paper will focus on persuasion, argument, or compare/contrast
11. Topic sentence must be clear and conclusion must reflect topic
12. Thesis statement must include all areas of concern for the given topic and must be conclusive in nature to be restated in final analysis of paper.
13. Reference page or work cite must be attached to paper
14. Title page and reference page (not counted in total pages).

TIMELINE: Project will be completed in a timely manner. The topic must reflect material presented in movie and/or textbook. A comparative summarization of all materials must be included in the final paper. Suggestions to follow standard writing format – for example, brainstorm, outline, draft, revision, proofread, listing of all major support, verify source, in-text citation must be utilized to avoid plagiarism. Please use a dictionary for correct spelling and pronunciations of words, spell checker, and grammarly. com or relevant grammar program found in "Word." Remember to read your work aloud for clarity; read your work backwards; if you have any questions or concerns, please email me.

Assessment and Grading

Upload Work to the Appropriate Area**

Writing Requirements (APA format) – Final Draft

- 3–5 pages (1500–2500 words)
- 1-inch margins
- Double-spaced
- 12-point Times New Roman font
- Cover page
- Reference page (2 must be correctly placed)
- Due date: Sunday before 11:59 p.m.

**Grading is 0% if no submission, else 50% on submission (50 points) – correct criterion will earn 50 points

Chapter 12

Issue in Literature – Fiction/Nonfiction

Common Terms in Literature – Reading that Novel

Allegory – narrative form in which characters are a representative of humanistic trait (greed, vanity)

Character – represented by a person, place, or thing performing human activities

Conflict – struggle between forces

Connotation – implied meanings

Denotation – words directly made in association with the meaning

Exposition – developing the background information regarding the setting, character, plot

Figurative – the use of words to express meaning beyond the literal

First person – all about me

Foreshadowing – writer clues to the reader that something is eventually going to occur

Hyperbole – exaggeration

Imagery – the author's attempt to create mental picture

Metaphor – contrasting to seemingly unalike things that have a common interest, to enhance the situation

Narrator – person telling the story

Omniscient – all knowing

Point-of-view – a story can sometimes indirectly establish the author's intention

Rhythm – often thought of the timing in a poem (allows the reader to move throughout the work)

Setting – the place or location for the action in a work typically provides historical or cultural context for the characters. In addition, could be symbolic of the "emotional state of the characters"

Simile – contrasting to seemingly unalike things that have a common interest, to enhance the meaning of a situation or themes using "like or as."

Symbolism – takes on an object meant to be representative of something or an idea greater than the object itself. For example – an owl will usually represent wisdom.

Third person – the story could be told from anyone's perspective

Discussion

In this course, we begin our journey through reading a novel, book, tradebook, or graphic novel collectively, as we are the readers. We must make adjustment in the speed at which we read the text. Using strategies for reading content will be of biggest help to develop stronger comprehension, vocabulary, and overall increase in your reading rate.

Initial Post (100 words)

Before we begin reading our book, please share with your classmates different strategies you like to do, while reading a book. For instance, on Saturday morning, I grab my favorite read for the month and I sit in the picture window. This is my "quiet area," and a place I am able to escape the daily routine. Remember to give as many details for your reading strategies as possible.

Secondary Posts (100 words each with at least two or more classmates)

Please reflect on your classmates strategies, there may be an "ah-ha moment," and you can make a connection. Better yet, you apply some of the strategies to your own. Remember to re-state the original post and support their claim with support from any of the readings, as the support makes your "opinion" stronger. Because remember that without support, your "opinion" means nothing in academics.

Writing Requirements

- Initial post length: 100 words
  - Due by Friday at 11:59 p.m.
- Secondary post length: Minimum of 100 words per post (respond to at least two classmates)
  - Due by Sunday at 11:59 p.m.

**Grading is 0% if no submission, or 10% for submission (10 points) – correct criterion will earn 10 points

Assignment – Vocabulary and the Final Stretch of Terms

Vocabulary and the Final Stretch of Terms

Just as the terms have been defined within the chapters, we must define "words" or vocabulary that we are unfamiliar with in the book. This will help to increase our reading rate, fluency, and comprehension as we embark on our new genre. Vocabulary throughout the entire book identified and recorded accurately and your habit to find new terms must remain consistent.

Therefore, similar to the vocabulary notebook created for our language development in an academic setting, this vocabulary will consist of **150 terms** that you are unfamiliar or unsure of the meaning of the word or term being used in the context, which they are read. Please know these new vocabulary words are for a grade, and will be collected at the end of the book, and returned as a graded assignment.

Specific directions will be given in the class. However, the final turn in of the notebook will reflect all vocabulary done in our course. Regardless of timeframe, these words will be reviewed upon submission and will contain **250 terms** that have the sentence in context to match the definition for the word.

Breakdown Review (word, definition, and sentences from the book)

Assimilation

Definition

Assimilation is the adoption or ways of another culture. For example, the language, of one culture, is resembling that of a different culture. Whereas, Franz, the German foreign exchange student, only spoke English in the classroom.

Another **fictitious** quote: "The assimilation of immigrants to America is overwhelming, as we are no longer considered a 'melting pot'" (Franks, 2011, p. 11).

Reading Fiction!

Chapter 13

Book or Trade book

How to Identify Meaningful Vocabulary

At the moment, anyone who reads the material, the need to understand the material increases, and the text explored must have fluency. Consequently, we come across unknown vocabulary, the comprehension ceases, and fluency interrupted for the moment. Ideally, there are reading strategies that you have been exposed to throughout this book, and the use of them will be crucial in your success to finish the novel in a timely manner.

Therefore, one of the best prereading strategies is to "walk through the book, text, or content" being introduced to the reader. Therefore, as the reader practices cursory reading, they will intentionally look for words within the text that should be unfamiliar, difficult to pronounce, or have been italicized for quick recognition. Identifying terms will help build background knowledge, and familiarity of unfamiliar words.

Next, create a list of unfamiliar words, and place the chapters or page numbers next to them. Then, begin to define them, once all the vocabulary are defined, cross-reference them if possible with annotation in the side margins or the annotation should be placed into the context for easier recall of the difficult words. Remember, all of these strategies take time, and practice will be the key to reading comprehension, fluency, and an increased reading rate.

The Model – Ready, Set, Read, Read, and Read as with practice; you will get better.

Jane and Sally are cutting across the grass; as Sally notices a man very **dapper** in style, and slows down to admire his attire.

STEP 1 – Recognize vocabulary

Dapper

STEP 2 – Define vocabulary

Dapper – to look stylish, well-dressed, fashionable

STEP 3 – Use the vocabulary in a sentence that represents the "meaning" of the vocabulary term

(Be careful, as there are several English vocabulary words, with multiple meanings)

Last fictitious EXAMPLE of Proper APA format

Jane and Sally are cutting across the grass; as Sally notices a man very **dapper** in style, and slows down to admire his attire (Frahn, 2014, p. 35). This is an example of copied directly from text to keep the context (meaning) the same. In addition, page 35 would reflect the word – **dapper** in the side margins of the text, along with the meaning found in the dictionary.

STEP 4 – Reread any text, which caused an interruption in the reading flow, as this will strengthen your comprehension.

STEP 5 – Recite any information aloud; this will ensure you have taken the vocabulary in the correct context. If context is incorrect, create a sentence of your own, reference the context cards developed earlier in the semester, and review annotation.

Discussion

For our book development, we are going to discuss some terms used in literature. As we are going to discuss the plot, setting, character development, and finally we should be at a point in our reading that reflects the "climax" of the book. This is the turning point in the story, as this book is unique and does reflect two "turning points," but only one is that pivotal moment where everything changes.

Initial Post (150–200 words)

Please chose one character, and it does not need to be the main character. Within your initial engagement, please give the character name, and the role you have established for the character within the storyline. In addition, give the "reader" as much background information, so that your interpretations will mirror each other, as closely as possible.

Establish the setting for the character; for example, Sally lives in the woods alone. Lastly, develop the plot for the reader, as this will be an interactive experience to guide both you and your peers to deduce and induce information from the story itself. Keep in mind, even though the use of visual aids is missing, the uses of descriptive vocabulary produce at times a more vivid "picture."

Secondary Posts (100 words each with at least two or more classmates)

Please review your peer's entries, and decide are you correctly interpreting the work of your peer. If you agree, please re-state their original post, and add an extension to make a continuum within our discussion board. The same criterion would hold true for a disagreement, always remember to "state the why."

Writing Requirements

- Initial post length: 150–200 words
  o Due by Friday at 11:59 p.m.
- Secondary post length: Minimum of 100 words per post (respond to at least two classmates)
  o Due by Sunday at 11:59 p.m.

**Grading is 0% if no submission, or 10% for submission (10 points) – correct criterion will earn 10 points

Week 14 – Assessment (25 total)

(This section is awarded 15 points)

1. Who is the author of the book?

2. How many pages you have to read for this week's assigned reading?

3. How does Ng (2014) treat time in the different "short stories" or chapters?

4. How does Ng (2014) use time in order to re-construct the past and discover the future?

5. Is this book an autobiography? If yes, why? If no, why?

6. How does this book compare to others in the same genre? What type of genre is this book?

7. What is the significance of being in the "middle" in the book? What is the significance of disappearing?

8. Ng (2014) says that an author touches on sensitive issues throughout the book and use symbols and exchanges with readers to come at various conclusions. Do you feel that you have connected in any way to the story? Could this be your story as well?

9. Are the book's themes relevant to your life?

10. Where does the author get the title of the book? Do the titles of chapters match the stories?

11. There are many references to saving people in the book ("Lydia saving herself," "The night saving a friend," "Jack saved Hannah from lying") – was there a "real" resolution? In other words, were these characters really being saved or just metaphorically speaking? (Explain in detail)

12. Who is the author (full name) and their role within the book? Does the author have a relationship to the main character?

13. How many pages you have to read? How many pages did you read? In other words, given and actually done.

14. Please give the name of the state these stories are based on occurring throughout the book, if you are able to give a fact you know about the state.

15. Did you ever encountered any emotions while reading these stories? If so what?

(Write at least three or more paragraphs)

16–25 (this section is awarded 10 points)

Give a description of Lydia and her view on relationships, and her relationships with her family. In addition, give a couple of examples that Ng (2014) used to describe the brother, the sister, and the friend (give their name).

*Please note this test may be given in class; therefore, please number your answers and make sure to re-state the question within the given answer to ensure a full understanding of the question.

Assignment – Rough Draft and Final Draft

Summary Essay Requirements and Basic Format

The Summary/Analysis Essay is based on the research you have found on your topic from the novel. You will write a draft, which you have made a connection from the one of the readings on "Pop Culture." Remember, your prewrite is the beginning stages to writing an essay. As you have done in class, the librarian taught you "how to" use the Ohiolink.

Please remember that you will need two outside resources for your Summary Essay draft.

The Ohiolink research is the material you will use in writing the rough draft, which later would become the final draft. Remember that each research piece that you use must be the in-text citation from the material in order to make a clear connection to your thoughts on a specific topic in pop culture. The best ways to organize these thoughts are given in these directions as it is broken down in an outline provided to you.

Being able to represent the ideas of others responsibly in your own writing is an important skill for academic writers. Therefore, in this assignment, we will be working to summarize an argument and to support that summary with well-chosen quotations and effective paraphrases. For this assignment, chose research, and read one of the genres that will match your topic. If you chose to find research that will take the opposite approach of your original work, you will support it the same way. Remember, you will be presenting in your writing the summary of the research.

For example – look at this fictitious work, Thursday seems to be the worst day on campus. According to Wong (2013), it has been found that Wednesday statistically appears to be worse, by almost "35%" (p. 3). Remember that you will introduce the "author" of your article, and the title of the article in your writing sample; thereafter, it is last name only with proper format. Be sure to "double check" your work for other's opinion. This will help to eliminate plagiarism.

Then, write a summary of your chosen essay supported by quotations and paraphrases of the text. Your task in this assignment is not to discuss your personal views on the subject, but to explain the views expressed by the author of your chosen text. Please make sure to use APA format, with proper in-text citations; in addition, create flow of the assignment with effective transitional words, or phrases. If you do not use the proper format, you risk plagiarism, be careful.

REMEMBER TO...

USE Prewriting

Read and re-read your chosen essay. As you read your work, highlight the main ideas and important examples in the text. Look for passages in which the writer explains his or her main conclusions. Try to talk to someone you know about the essay. Work to explain the main idea in your own words after reading the essay. This practice will help you organize your thoughts and find the words you need to explain the ideas you read about.

Outline

Make an outline that lists for yourself to review the main arguments and important supporting examples of the essay. Particularly, as you begin drafting your essay, you can refer back to and draw from this outline to help you shape your first draft. If you utilize a list, please make sure to write down the "sentence" and page number, this will help you with proper in-text citation, as you will know "where" the information for support came from in the original work.

Drafting and Revisions

In your paper explain the main idea discussed in your chosen essay. Be sure to explain in detail only the most important supporting details. Remember that your target audience includes individuals who have probably not read the essay that you have chosen to summarize. Therefore, it is your responsibility to provide the background information and context for your discussion of the major claims and examples of the text.

Guidelines to Write this Summary

The Summary/Analysis form of writing is an essay style that is frequently used in academic writing, and mastering this form of composition is critical to success, certainly in English courses, but in other academic disciplines as well. As the name suggests, the goal of this type of writing is to summarize an assigned piece of writing – whether it is an opinion essay, an academic journal article, a work of short fiction, or some other form of writing – and then analyze that piece of writing, informing your audience of your position on the issue being raised.

Beginning the first element of Summary/Analysis writing is to inform your audience, generally, what you think an author is saying in an assigned essay or article. This is the summary. Remember: your goal is NOT to retell, in blow-by-blow fashion, line-by-line from material the author has written, but rather to identify generally the high points and your interpretation of the author's piece.

Consequently, the second element of Summary/Analysis writing is to establish for your audience your position on the issue raised in the assigned essay. Think in these terms, do you agree (for) or disagree (against) with the author's position, and why? And while you will not use the first person "I" in this essay, you will be making clear what you believe to be valid or invalid about the what the author has to say by using declarative sentences (facts – directly stated within the reading). Remember not to do just a restatement of the assigned reading, you must present your position for or against the given work you are summarizing within your writing sample.

Organizational Format: (Basic Outline Format BASED ON THEMES)

I. **Introductory paragraph** – Should NOT refer to the assigned essay.

Instead, it should focus generally on the issue raised in the essay. The introduction should reflect an anecdote, either personal or third person, which can relate to the subject to be discussed. For example, a statistic that you can relate to the subject; a fact that you can relate to the subject; a quote from either a famous person or someone nonfamous, that you can relate to the overall idea or topic/subject; or a question that functions as a lead-in to your discussion of the essay.

II. Summary paragraph – Should begin with the sentences reflecting title of work and authors name

*Based on (author's name must go here – do not use parenthesis) "title of work must be placed in quotation marks" presents the following…Based on **Ng (2014) "Everything I Never Told You"**

*"Title of work must be placed in quotation marks" as (author's name must go here – do not use parenthesis) provided several insights to … **"Everything I Never Told You" as Ng (2014) provided**

Furthermore, you should finish this sentence with a general statement of what main point – or thesis – you believe the author is making with his essay. This is the controlling theme for your entire analysis of his essay, so it must be clear. However, you will NOT use specific examples from the essay in this paragraph; rather, you will speak generally about the author's thesis. This is the interpretation of their work, and you are presenting it based on your background knowledge for the reader. **For example, according to Ng (2014), life was full of disappointments, such as their race, their parent's religion, and even disappointment in marriage.**

III. (Body) A "sub-theme" (topic idea) paragraph – (each example or topic will require its own paragraph, depending upon the detail and development of an individual example, two or three paragraphs may be required to cover a single topic) Use words like "for instance" or "for example" or "another example offered." However, you will use specific examples from the essay in this paragraph.

A. PROVIDE **Examples**

B. GIVE A SPECIFIC **Topic** with support from text

IV. Analysis paragraph(s)

Your analysis/opinion of the theme. In this paragraph, you state what you think about the author's point. Refer to specific examples as needed. You must include paraphrased and quoted material with proper in-text citation using the APA formatted style of writing.

V. (Body) A "sub-theme" (topic idea) paragraph – (each example or topic will require its own paragraph, depending upon the detail and development of an individual example, two or three paragraphs may be required to cover a single topic). Use words like "for instance" or "for example" or "another example offered." However, you will use specific examples from the essay in this paragraph.

A. PROVIDE Examples

B. Again PROVE the Topic with support from text

VI. Analysis paragraph(s)

Your analysis/opinion of theme #2. In this paragraph, you state what you think about the author's point. Refer to specific examples as needed. You must include paraphrased and quoted material with proper in-text citation using the APA formatted style of writing.

VII. Summary Conclusion

In this paragraph, you should re-state or sum up in a few sentences the author's main point; reiterating, in a couple/few sentences, the conclusions YOU have drawn about the essay. Finalizing support presented in the summary to leave the reader with a complete picture of your interpretation or analysis of the material being presented in your essay. The **conclusion** is closure to the argument by explaining "why" the argument is important, or by discussing the implications of the argument.

Assessment and Grading

Upload Work to the Appropriate Area**

Writing Requirements (APA format)

- 2–3 pages (approx. 300 words per page)
- 1-inch margins
- Double-spaced
- 12-point Times New Roman font
- 2 resources from the Ohiolink data base
- Cover page
- Reference page (must reflect the Ohiolink Sources: No Wikipedia)
- Rough draft due date: Sunday by 11:59 p.m.
- Final draft due date: Last Week of Classes Friday by 11:59 p.m.

**Grading is 0% if no submission, or 25% for submission (25 points) – correct criterion will earn 25 points

Evaluating Text

Summary of this Text

As our semester comes to a close, a few terms have to be reviewed before we leave each other. Overall, the purpose of a summary comprised a paragraph or two that will reflect solely on the main idea, or claim specified in the reading, article, or "multigenre" piece of literary composition; always cite the title and the author or authors. Moreover, a summary is rewritten into your own wording to express your interpretation of the "main idea"; however, if you reiterate the "central theme" based on the "author's" perspective, utilize statistical information, re-create an idea based as if you "were there," or any other knowledge, which "will not be considered" common fact, or knowledge.

Additionally, as a "writer," you should be thoughtful, positive, creative, and even logical in your approach. As you evaluate critique, analyze, comment on, or review another, you should produce relevance, credibility, and reliability to your writing sample. Regardless, you must use in-text citations to give credit to the source or sources, as you must give "credit where credit is due." Consequently, information to keep in mind as you are creating your summary: first be effective, as you produce effectiveness you will reinforce basic reading strategies, such as identifying common themes or ideas (denotation, connotation), reading critically (inductive and/or deductive logic), and comprehension.

Secondly, as you change the wording, "do not change" the author's original intension or interpretation of material presented to the reader, whereas misinterpretation will create a lack of understanding of the original piece. Importantly, all academic works unless otherwise specified will remove your opinion from the interpretations, therefore writing samples are based solely on interpretation of the reader and supported with "facts," which must contain proper in-text citation. Finally, all writing samples should be in "third person," leave "I" out of it, as you are very important; "I" should not be the "center" or "focus" of the summary.

Lastly, the summary should be based only on the information presented to the reader; "your background knowledge" will be used for other literary interpretations. Therefore, "stick to the piece"; consequently, the summary length should consist of a shortened version, not ever longer than the original work or source. Following these strategies and guidelines (tips) in several ways will help produce an effective writer.

Topics Throughout the Course

Discussion 1 – APA format (readings require in-text citations)

Initial post (150–200 words)

For this week's discussion board, the initial post will be a reflection of the semester. As you begin to write, reflect on the beginning of the semester, work assignments, deadlines, guidelines, and particularly, the readings. As you moved to the middle, again please reflect on the same topics. As this course comes to a close, reflect on topics, readings, and the like, which you feel should still be covered or reviewed before your final days. Please remember to stay as objective as possible, however as you are expressing emotions, which are pure "feelings" to stay positive.

Secondary Posts: (100 words each peer response with at least two or more classmates)

Will answer the basic questions that follow as a guideline, and you are more than welcome to add any interaction, which you feel will create a continuum of the discussion board. Remember to engage with at least two or more classmates in the discussion board. Thank you for your hard work, diligence, and dedication to your education, as well as to your peers.

For the interaction, please give your peer the following feedback:

1. Could you relate to your peer?
2. Did you have similar feelings toward this course?
3. Were your expectations met?
4. Did you learn anything?
5. Give an example if you find something in common with your peer…for example, as I began this course I was not sure I would be able to pass; however, I knew if I put my mind to it, I would be fine.

Writing Requirements – See Rubric

- Initial post length: 150–200 words
  - Due by Wednesday at 11:59 p.m.
- Secondary post length: Minimum of 100 words per post (respond to at least two classmates)
  - Due by Sunday at 11:59 p.m.

**Grading is 0% if no submission, or 10% for submission (10 points) – correct criterion will earn 10 points

Assessment

Book or Tradebook

"Everything I Never Told You" 20 points

Define the words…and (total of 10 points)

1. homogeneous-

2. mongrel -

3. patriarchy -

4. brooding-

5. discernible-

6. gerrymandering-

7. gregarious-

8. ambiguity –

9. scrounge-

10. phony-

Use the words in a sentence…one word per sentence…

1.

2.

3.

4.

5.

6.

7.

8.

9.

10.

Rewrite the ending (total of 10 points)… ("Everything I Never Told You")

(Must be at least 2–3 paragraphs)

Give your opinion of the book… this is a critique "book review"

Due date: Final day of class

Please copy and paste your answers into a "Word document." Upload no later than Sunday at 11:59 p.m.

References

Allington, R. L. (1984). Content coverage and contextual reading in reading groups. *Journal of Reading Behavior, 16*, 85–96.

Atwan, R. (2013). *America now: short readings from recent periodicals* (10th ed). Boston: Bedford/St. Martin's.

Barrs, M. (2000). The reader in the writer. *Reading.* 54–60.

Bartholomae, D. (1986). Inventing the university. *Journal of Basic Writing 5*(1), 4–23.

Bloom, B. (1956). *Bloom's taxonomy of learning domains.* Retrieved from https://www.nbna.org/files-BloomsTaxonomyLearning.pdf

Carr, S. C. & Thompson, B. (1996). The effects of prior knowledge and schema activation strategies on the inferential reading comprehension of children with and without learning disabilities. *Learning Disability Quarterly, 19*, 48–61.

Cunningham, A. E., & Stanovich K. E. (1998). What reading does for the mind. *American Educator, 22*(1 & 2), 8–15.

Cunningham, P., Cunningham, J., Allington, R., & Hall, D. (2002). *Research on the Components of a Comprehensive Reading and Writing Instructional Program.* Retrieved from www.uvm.edu/~cdci/tripscy/localpdf/Literacy_Websites.doc

Ghuman, S. (2012). "Is technology destroying social bonds." *Technology Hurts Social Bonds.* In Atwan, R. (2013). *America now: short readings from recent periodicals* (10th ed).Boston: Bedford/St. Martin's. 110–111.

Joseph, L.(2007). Understanding, assessing, & intervening on reading problems.

Landsberger, J. (1996). Study guide and strategies. *Study Guides and Strategies Website.* Retrieved from https://www.studygs.net

Merriam-Webster. (2017) Definition of assimilate. Retrieved from: https://www.merriam-webster.com/dictionary/assimilate

Mosher, D. (2012, February 24). Easily pronounced names make people more likable. *Wired Science.* Retrieved from: https://www.wired.com/2012/02/name-pronunciation-success/

National Association of School Psychologists. 15–35. NASP. ISBN: 9780932955-76-0. Retrieved from: http://www.nasponline.org/publications/booksproducts/reading_001.pdf

Ousborne, J. (2013). *Reading pop culture: a portable anthology.* New York: Bedford/St. Martin's.

Service-Learning Course Design Workbook. (2001). *Adapted from the* Michigan Journal of Community Service Learning. OCSL Press, Summer 2001, The University of Michigan.

Stanley, B. (1904). *Success.* Retrieved from http://www.symphonyoflove.net/blog/1390/success-by-bessie-anderson-stanley.html

Stolley, K., Brizee, A. & Paiz, J. (2013). Is it plagiarism yet? *Purdue OWL.* Retrieved from: https://owl.english.purdue.edu/owl/resource/589/02/

Toledo Area Humane Society (TAHS). (2017). Adopt a pet. Retrieved from: https: www. toledohumane.org.

List of Readings

Chapter 2

Barthes, Roland (1972) "Toys" [translated]

Bartholomae, David (1986) "Inventing the University"

Mosher, Dave (2012) "Easily Pronounced Names May Make People More Likeable"

Chapter 3

Lutz, William (1989) "With these Words I Can Sell You Anything"

Chapter 4

Bryson, Bill (1994) "Made in America" *Hard Sell: Advertising in America*

Fletcher, Winston (2008) "Art or Puffery"

Chapter 5

Christian, Aymar Jean (2011) "The Problem of YouTube"

Chapter 7

Moss, Michael (2013) "The Extraordinary Science of Junk Food"

Mullich, Joe (2013) "Should We Eat by the Numbers"

Chapter 9

Johnson, Steven (2005) "Watching Television Makes You Smarter"

Will, George (2001) "Reality Television Oxymoron"

Chapter 12

Hsu, Hua (2009) "The End of White America"

Chapter 13

Ng, Celeste (2014) "Everything I Never Told You"

CPSIA information can be obtained
at www.ICGtesting.com
Printed in the USA
FFHW011016170719
53688716-59363FF